RIDE IT!

The Complete Book of
MOTORCYCLE TRIALS

Don Smith
edited by Graham Forsdyke of *Motor Cycle*

Printed in England for the publishers by
J. H. Haynes and Company Limited
Sparkford Yeovil Somerset England

The Haynes Publishing Group
Sparkford Yeovil Somerset BA22 7JJ England

A FOULIS MOTORCYCLING BOOK - ISBN 0 85429 165 2

Distributed in North America by
Haynes Publications Inc.
861 Lawrence Drive
Newbury Park
California 91320

Telephones: (213) 889 - 5400   (805) 498 - 6703

Editor Jeff Clew
Production/Design Tim Parker
Illustration Terry Davey

RIDE IT!
The Complete Book of Motorcycle Trials

DON SMITH

edited by Graham Forsdyke

Foreword

No one man could have written a foreword to a book by Don Smith. For the Londoner who has travelled the world spreading the trial-riding gospel, is an almost professional collector of friends. Each he leaves with a deep impression of his sincerity and, above all, his dedication to the past-time which, for him, started as a sport and turned into a business.

Faced with a problem of finding an author for this introduction, I finally came up with the idea of a combination job, composed of various comments from some of those who have got to know Don during his riding career.

Like 1973 British and European Champion Martin Lampkin who calls him "the most competent ambassador our sport has ever had". Martin first met Don on the ferry en route to an Irish Hurst Cup Trial. "I wanted to know who the flamboyant, friendly character was and Peter Gaunt told me, adding that Don had tried his hand at most things — including pop singing — usually with great success. Now that he has written a book on his favourite subject, I am convinced that it will be a success, having the utmost confidence in his ability to pass on his knowledge to a wider audience."

Some riders have clearly defined memories of the sportsmanship that Don is capable of displaying. Yamaha's Mick Andrews will never forget the 1962 Scottish Six Days Trial when the oil tank of his 350 cc AJS split on the final run into Edinburgh. "I was lying second to Sammy Miller at the time with Don in third spot only a mark or two behind. The oil tank problem, if it were noticed at the final inspection, would have clocked up sufficient penalty marks to swap Don and I in the results. When he saw my problem, instead of thanking heaven for his luck, he set to with a rag to help me clear the tell-tale oil from the machine before it was handed in. Don could have won the Scottish that year for Sammy Miller had also had trouble with a cracked frame which had to be secretly welded. Had the organisers been aware of this and my tank trouble, Don would have been promoted to winner."

But it's not only the riders that Don influences in the same way. Sam Tanegashima, marketing manager of the mighty Engine and Motor Cycle division of Kawasaki Heavy Industries tells of Don's first visit to Japan. "Of the hundreds of foreign visitors who come to Kawasaki, none ever stayed at the local hotel which, although only half a mile away, is pure Japanese with no concessions to Western visitors. Guests always opt for another, American-style hotel 18 miles distant. But not Don. Declaring that he had come to work anyway he settled in at the local hotel, got the friendly nick-name 'crazy Don' and, within a week, had them making tea, English-style. Now he's a guest of honour on every trip he makes."

Suzuki ace Gordon Farley has known Don for 13 years and is particularly impressed with his attention to detail. "Don always dresses perfectly whether attending a club dinner or working on his bike in the garage. But, what always gets me is his uncanny ability to get others to understand his requirements — even in a foreign country where the language barrier would overcome lesser men. He gets the same thing across in this book — it's a must to be owned by enthusiasts everywhere."

We'll let America have the last word. To be precise, Pete Nelson of the Los Angeles Police Department — a man who Don insists on calling Colombo. The two met in early 1974 at the first American round of the world championships which Pete helped to organise. And Colombo needs little excuse to talk of Don's enthusiasm which he calls "his most valuable asset and makes him unique amongst his peers. Few really appreciate the part he has played in expanding trials throughout the world. In this book he tells it how it really is — I only wonder that he has waited so long to put it all down on paper."

Graham Forsdyke
Administration and Production
Editor of *Motor Cycle*

with help from
Martin Lampkin
Mick Andrews
Sam Tanegashima
and Pete Nelson

Contents

Introduction

Don Smith is a character - in a sport which, by its very nature, breeds characters.

To stand out from the crowd in such company, a man must have a lot more going for him than simply to be able to ride a bike well.

And the Don Smith I have known since our schooldays is just such an extrovert, making friends with a brash approach which, in other men, would be labelled pure exhibitionism.

Since those early days we have both gone our own ways in the world of two wheels; he as a trials superstar and myself as a journalist following his exploits across the world.

For we are both mixed up with motorcycles. Trials machines have a strange, indefinable quality which can grip you young and hold your interest until your dotage. And Don knows the motorcycle game backwards, forwards and inside out. What's more, his enthusiasm for the sport is infectious, as all those who read this book will discover.

As a teacher, at the many trials schools he has organised all over the world, he excels, giving novice riders the benefit of his 23 years' experience in the game, and as a friend rather than a remote schoolmaster.

And it's this same gift for passing on knowledge and experience that comes across in this book. But be warned; if you don't like bikes, can't stand getting dirty, or already tie up all your free time with another pursuit, don't read on. For Don, in this book, will grab you and turn you into an enthusiast — well before you've reached the last page.

Graham Forsdyke
Administration and Production
Editor of *Motor Cycle*

1
The Trials game

Picture the scene, the entire family out for the day, the car parked by a stream on a little patch of land. Mum, dad and the kids enjoying themselves on the bike, never out of visual distance of the baby. Don't ask me why I love trials, the answer's obvious.

How else for a minimal outlay can the whole family get such a good-fun deal? The sport of trials is a practical proposition for everyone. Executives to farm labourers, bankers to road-menders — all can get the same kicks, the same healthy deal — and on a trials bike they are all equal.

We're not talking about a temperamental, high-stressed piece of machinery, needing the constant attention of a mechanic with near brain surgeon experience. Today's bike is the result of years of engineering experience and, for anyone wanting to join in this sport, is virtually maintenance free.

You'd be surprised at how the little work that is necessary is just plain fun. The small price to pay for all that sport is the weekly wash off, and odd running adjustment.

For the serious competitor, who has established himself, there are even more bonuses. He will travel the world, and between events, ski in the Swiss mountains, see Monte Carlo by night, storm passes in the Alps, sunbathe on the Mediterranean coast, and, all the while, enjoy the hospitality that fellow trials riders extend to their friends all over the globe.

I've never been against, either, signing autographs to the hordes of girls who seem to pop up, as if by magic, at every event. And, if you turn out good enough, it can mean spending most of your teens and twenties doing what you like doing best and getting paid handsomely for it.

I'm not going to try to put any date on just when trials started, for the sport of getting from A to B across obstacles was born when the first motorcycles were built in backyards all over the world.

This golden oldie is a flash-back to 1926. Note the footing coat and the size of that crowd!

With those primitive bikes, often with but one gear and a slipping canvas-and-rubber belt providing the drive to a narrow-section rear tyre, any trip was an adventure.

And when you add to that mixture, the indifferent dirt roads full of pot-holes and wash-outs, it's obvious that no journey could be undertaken lightly. Man and machine were united in a bid to overcome the problems of surface and gradient just as they are in an observed trial today.

For the fun in pitting yourself against a difficult hazard hasn't changed.

Early organised trials in the 1920s were long-distance affairs where hills were featured with marks gained for non-stop climbs. Many of those self-same hills are still in use today. But now, with decent surfaces, they form parts of normal roads. Although the fierceness of their gradients may not have been eased, the modern machine - or the family car for that matter - has no difficulty in surmounting them.

From all this, the modern trials machine evolved. Because of the very nature of the sport, the bike is a highly specialised machine - but also quiet, light, slim and designed to inspire confidence.

Trials bikes compare with motocross, road-racing and speedway machines, as does a soft family dog with a fighting bull. Anyone, but anyone, can ride a trials bike. It takes a particular breed to come to grips with a snorting, purpose-built racer.

While a trials bike can provide fun for a complete family, there's no way that an untractable racer can do the same for a group of all ages and both sexes.

This fun begins the day the bike arrives in the family garage, and without even starting the engine.

Balance is all important in the trials game, so why not let the first family contest start right there and then? The whole group can each stand on the footrest pegs for as long as possible with who-does-the-washing-up as the loser's penalty.

Amanda's just six and it'll be a while before she goes the solo route - at least on a bike this big

You'll have big trouble keeping the kids off your trials bike. This is Karen, who is ten. First stage is to drive the bike with her sitting in the riding position and just holding onto the bars

Stage two. We are progressing, but I am running alongside just in case we hit trouble

Sounds tame? Don't you believe it. That's a game you'll come back to time and again. I still do and that's after 23 years in the trials game.

The next step in getting acquainted with the bike still need not take you out of the home area.

Half a dozen bricks laid in a line along the driveway give you the simplest section. Just ride in and out of them in the same way as a skier performs his stunts. But, for this version, you don't need the snow slalom, the slope of the usually-necessary long trip. Trials bike fun is instant.

Getting a little proficient at the brick game? Learning about the use of brakes, clutch, throttle, and how the bike responds to your slightest body movement? Alright. Now try moving the bricks a little closer together. It's just become difficult again. And how about climbing up over every third brick? The possibilities are endless, so is the enjoyment factor.

Trials is a game, a sport, that can be tackled in easy stages. When the driveway has been exhausted there's the rest of the country to be explored.

You don't need much ground to practice this manoeuvre. Only props are a few bricks. What you'll learn is throttle, clutch and brake control plus a good bit about balance.

The same performance, only this time I'm using concrete posts. Almost anything can be utilised to form a trials section

One word of caution. Trials is by far the safest of all forms of motorcycle sport, but, like everything else, a complete lack of common-sense can lead to the odd minor injury. What is important is to take things gently. At a big international event you will watch the superstars launching their machines over near precipices. Don't try to emulate them straight away. You'll scare yourself and there's no sense in that.

Without exception those superstars started out just as you will do. They have graduated to the big-time and play big-time tricks for big-time money. If you want to graduate from the family fun scene to the world of competition it's a thing to be done in easy stages.

Learning about trials, the machines and the ground over which they travel will teach a lot more besides.

If I had my way, trials would be taught in schools. It's the greatest possible aid to road safety. When I hear drivers explaining accidents in which they say *the steering just went*, I simply wince. What they are saying really is that the road surface changed, the wheels skidded and they hadn't the faintest idea what to do about it.

A youngster brought up in a trials atmosphere and learning to ride a machine, knows all about recognising changes of surface. Instinctively he sees them, feels them and, just as important, knows what to do about them.

Now, I'm a nervous passenger. I cringe at the very thought of someone giving me a practical demonstration of just what a good driver he is. But, take it from me, if I know my driver is a trials man, the panic barometer slides down to the calm level.

So what have we got?

The sport of trials is a full-family deal, safe, a healthy outdoor pastime with dozens of off-shoot bonuses.

Can you wonder I'm hooked on it?

Use this book to approach the sport properly and share this fun with me.

As I've said, superstars get quite a bit of fun -- apart from trials riding. This is Spanish champion Randy Munoz during an off-moment.

2
What is trials?

One of my prize possessions, on the wall of my den, is a pin-up Kawasaki poster of an extremely-well-endowed female member of the Japanese company's American promotion team. We got to be friends during one of my trips to the States and, before the first American round in the world championship series, she gave me the poster with a good luck message written on the bottom.

But, despite the sentiment and the obvious charm of the picture, I wince every time I look at it. For she had written *Best of luck in the trials*. It drives me mad. Perhaps it's an irrational thing but I get considerably uptight at the inaccurate use of the words trial and trials.

I ride a **trials bike** and compete in a **trial**. I do not ride a trial bike and compete in the trials.

A covy of Kwackers -- myself and works rider Richard Sunter -- take a breather during a practice session

To the uninitiated, the mere phrase 'motorcycle trials' can conjure up a vast variety of pictures. And, with some reasons for, as this sport of ours evolved, trials have developed a series of off-shoots. Some concentrate on speed, some on the ability of man and machine to overcome obstacles and others on long-distance endurance.

I've concentrated my life around one particular aspect of our sport — the one we discussed in the first chapter. The one that gives sport to all.

Right, let's pin down just what an observed trial is all about. We're talking about a group of riders — anything from two to 200 — and a series of obstacles over, or through, which the bikes must be ridden. Ideally, in each section the contestants will start and go through to the finish without stopping, without putting a foot down to aid balance, and without paddling (also called legging or footing) with the feet if the rear tyre runs out of grip.

Penalties are given for anything short of an ideal performance and these can vary from event to event.

In England, one trial called, appropriately enough, the 'Do or Die' has stayed popular with its extremely rare marking system. In it, riders who get through a section with their feet still on the pegs, amass no penalty. And it's the competitor who manages the greatest number of penalty-free sections, who takes the premier award.

The advantages of this system are few and the score against the scheme is considerable.

Trials are not, and should not be, a bull-in-a-china shop affair and, although such a set-up eases the problems for those working out the results, rider-finesse goes out of the window when a man is just asked to aim his bike at a section and not fall off before he's passed the 'ends' card.

Any decent section presents a variety of hazards and is in itself, a collection of problems. Under the 'Do or Die' set-up, if the rider has to put a foot down early on in the section, he immediately fails and has no interest in the rest of the section.

For this reason the 1-3-5 system, which was almost universally used until the 1970s, has considerable advantages. Under it a rider loses one mark if he puts a foot to the ground just once. Anything more than once increases the penalty to three. A five is scored for a complete stop, riding outside the marked boundaries or for knocking down any of the boundary markers.

This marking method obviously does away with some of my criticisms of the 'Do or Die' set-up — but only some of them.

There is still the problem of the rider who puts a foot down early on in the section and then, with a first-class performance, gets through the rest of the hazard but has one more quick prod at the very end. It could have been a top-quality ride, perhaps the best by any competitor in the event, but it earned him the same penalty as the man who started legging his way before he even got into the section and disappears out of sight still footing.

Also the man who has two steadying prods early on, has little incentive to do anything other than leg his way through the rest of the section.

Recently the 1-2-3-5 system has been tried. This provides for the rider who has just two prods by penalizing him two marks. In other respects it is the same as the earlier 1-3-5 set-up.

More and more organisers are going over to this later system. For, although it means more work for the observers who note each rider's performance, and the results team who collate and work out the finishing order, it gives a better indication of rider ability. Another advantage of the system is that, from a spectator's point of view, the rider keeps on trying.

I sometimes think that a more elaborate system could be evolved to give a greater advantage to the man with a faultless performance but the greater the number of marking alternatives, the more chance of confusion and differences of opinion.

Trials are a simple, friendly sport and, perhaps on balance (no pun intended), we'd better leave things as they are.

It is usual to have some system for deciding ties. There are quite a few alternatives, including the winner being the man with the greatest number of clean rides in the sections or the man who went furthest round the course without losing marks. In that order they are the systems I prefer.

Some trials even use a timed section for the elimination but I'm not keen on that idea. For, to my mind, a short bit of motocross has no place in the middle of a trial.

Enduros have much more relationship to **trail** work than to **trials** riding and are run over vast areas of land, with speed and regularity the prime objects.

The trials game is certainly an all-weather sport and, yes, that's snow on the ground. I must have been particularly determined that day for I'm not even wearing gloves

When the class of event gets to the international status, the organisers are not over-worried about just what they send you through on the first day. This fearsome rockery, aptly named Edramucky, regularly faces competitors on the opening run of the Scottish Six Days Trial

The grand-daddy of all enduros — the International Six Days Trial — is held every year with countries entering national teams in a fierce 1000-mile event with long speed tests used to sort out the winners.

Such races and the American Baja and Mint events do not really come within the compass of this book, nor does the sport of trail riding and its British equivalent — green-roads riding.

Not that all observed trials are one-day affairs. In Britain, two-day events are quite commonplace and, of course, we have the most famous trial of all, the Scottish Six Days, using sections in the Western Highlands. The multi-day trial is obviously the thing of the future. Spain has already held a three-day event and similar competitions in America are inevitable.

If you've read this far through the book, it could well be that you are getting tempted towards joining me in my sport and wondering whether it's possible to go trials riding on your current machine. Regrettably the answer is probably no — unless you are already lucky enough to have a genuine trials bike lurking in the garage. I'll modify that — it is possible to go trials riding on anything with wheels but I'm talking about the maximum enjoyment that can only come using the correct tool for the job.

Perhaps a cross-country, off-road trail bike, ideal for exploring lanes, comes nearest to a trials machine but very soon the limitations become obvious. You'll soon discover that the footrests are in the wrong position, ground clearance under the engine is inadequate, steering lock insufficient, gearing is wrong and a dozen other little items that will eliminate the machine for serious trials use.

Trying to ride trials on a trail bike will dent you mentally and physically. You'll have trouble in cleaning the simplest trial sections and find that you're doing an awful lot of unnecessary hard work. On a trail machine you'll find what a motorcycle can't do. A trials machine shows just what is possible.

What we've got here is a very pretty picture taken in a stream bed never before used in trials. Such rocks are often covered with slime...   *....... as you can see*

I strongly advise the owner of a trail bike to ride out and find himself some sections. Try the hazards and realise the failings of the bike, for the job it is being asked to do. Before he knows it, that same man will be off to his nearest dealer to talk trade-in for a thoroughbred trials lump. And once he gets it, and finds that same section again, everything will have changed. As if by magic, what was difficult will turn into a main-road drive and what was impossible will no longer be so. That's the secret ingredient of trials — the flavour that becomes an intoxicant — the sense of achievement that stems from a successful ride over, as ability grows, increasingly difficult obstacles.

And look at the side benefits that come from the ownership of a trials bike. The civilised machine can be used for trailing, commuting to work or just slipping around to the corner shop for groceries — and, again, it's a bike that all the family can use.

But trailmen have done trials riders one great service. Forced with the demand by motor-cyclists for open ground on which to play, two distinct things are happening in America. On one hand the Government is recognising the demand and scheduling vast areas of land to be designated as motorcycle areas. And promoters are developing enormous parks as two-wheel playgrounds. I've been to many such parks and to an Englishman they are mind-blowing. In fact, the man from Britain could be completely misled by the term 'park'. Forget your local corporation recreation ground. Think instead in terms of parks as big as British counties.

The great off-shoot of all this is enough sections to last the world a lifetime. And, as the great trials boom sweeps on, more and more facilities will be laid on for the feet-up enthusiast. I can foresee a great series of land areas spreading across the country where the family can go for a trials evening, day or weekend. And, in the same way as golf courses work, each trials area will have its own resident professional to pass on the finer points of the art. And the glory of it all is that the actual area of land needed is so small. In England complete trials are held in super small areas, some only the size of a football stadium.

I have pioneered the idea of motorcycle playground in England with Linford Park in Essex. Here I set out to provide a complete adventure ground for two-wheel enthusiasts and I see the day when such places are as easy to find as the local bowling alley or golf course.

But, although such commercial areas can provide much-appreciated fringe benefits — refreshments, washing facilities etc — a trials ground is where you find it and it's plenty easy to find.

Trials, still in their infancy as a spectator sport, are certain to become one of the nation's fastest-growing attractions. The ice was really broken early in 1974 in Goteborg, Sweden, where the first ever international indoor event was held.

This was a real circus-type promotion, where the world's best riders were ferried over on special charter aircraft by the organisers who provided them with bikes of their own choosing, and, as an added incentive, lucrative prize money for the winners.

The event was just like a show-jumping contest with imaginative artificial hazards built up by the organisers. Sections included riding along a 30 ft by 4 inch wide plank — just the width of the rear wheel — and climbing up onto a table, turning through 180° and climbing down again.

Make no mistake about it, in the not-too-distant future such events will become commonplace throughout the world.

3
Types of event

The art of competition riding in trials encompasses the full spectrum of the sport, from the family fun in the driveway to full-blooded international competition where world professional riders vie with each other for the valuable prizes to be won.

Make no mistake about it, for the handful of superstars the returns are considerable. It's all there — the mind-blowing retainer figures paid by factories to tempt the top men, press coverage, bonus payments from accessory manufacturers and jet trips all over the world from one venue to another to be treated with filmstar welcomes.

But it's a cold hard world, the one of the professional rider. The family fun thing disappears when the need to pay the bills comes in.

Perhaps I'm being over cynical for I've been lucky enough to have a certain ability which has let me do what I like, and glory, glory, to be paid well for doing it. To some, all the fun disappears from the sport when professionalism takes over but, again, I've been lucky. Every now and again I push the thought of next week's big event aside, ignore the inevitable giant pile of paperwork that's part of running a trials team and, instead, hitch the bike onto the car and head out with the family to a quiet spell of enjoying what I like best.

But we are talking about the one in 10,000 who decided to make a living out of the sport. For the other 9,999 the game remains a progressing fun thing.

Let me explain what I mean. There you are, you've bought a trials bike, gone through the balancing in the garage bit, played in the drive and are now heading out to open country every chance you have. Now, how long before your neighbour begins to wonder about that stark two-wheeler he sees slung across the rear of your car each weekend? You tell him and it's not long before good neighbour, Bill, is in the passenger seat of your car with you to see just what all the fuss is about. At your favourite trials ground he watches you perform. He's mildly interested so you let him try the bike on an easy banking — you're not worried, the bike is near indestructible.

Bill probably makes one hell of a hash of the deal so you pass on a little of your hard-earned expertise. He does a little better and suddenly you've got a convert.

I can guarantee to take any fun-loving, open-minded individual, give him an hour's tuition on a trials bike and convert the man into an enthusiast. Such is the lure of trials.

But back to Bill. All the way home he's talking about bikes and at the first opportunity, you take him and his family down to your friendly dealer. Now he's got a bike and a whole new social scene opens up. Daylight leisure hours are spent riding the bikes and the evenings become sessions for both families, re-living the events of the day and planning the next trip.

But, could be, your earlier start in the game is still giving you the edge over Bill and, perhaps, even your wife can put him down. That's when the good neighbour gets sneaky and slides off for what he calls a business trip. When he and his family get back — what kind of business trip takes in the whole group? — suddenly he's a lot, lot better and you are the underdog.

What he has done is to slope off to one of the many trials schools which are being held all over. Here top-class riders pass on the benefits of their knowledge to local riders. And, believe me, it works given a good teacher, and a pupil who really wants to learn.

I foresee a complete line of trials schools springing up all across the country where the resident pro will be ready to give out with the knowledge, pinpoint and cure the odd fault and foible that anyone teaching themselves a new sport develops.

OK, so now you've tumbled his advantage and had a little tuition of your own and, even if you say it yourself, you are getting pretty damn good at this trials game. The pair of you are ready to graduate to a little competition.

As the man nearly said, *a little proficiency is a dangerous thing*. I know, I've experienced the same deal.

Back in my 'teens I was the local hotshot. I knew it. After all, I was going out to small local events week after week and winning them all. It was all getting a little monotonous — almost a bore. So this big fish in his little pool decided the time was ripe to swim out and show the world just what an ace he was.

God, I made a fool of myself.

I chose an event in the Midlands of England and, with the then current superstars that I was so easily going to put down, came up to Hawks Nest — a giant rocky eruption conceived by nature on a very off day!

They had to be joking. No one, but no one, bar a mountain goat complete with rope and alpenstock was ever going to get up that rock face.

But the superstars did and with style, placing their wheels within a couple of inches of their chosen paths. I was sick, really sick. That big super ego went flat. Instantly.

This is the fearsome sight that faced me when I first left my little pool to vie with Britain's top riders on rocky sections -- one of the most sobering experiences of my life

The same thing may well happen to you and Bill in your first event. As we've said, you feel you are ready and that local dealer starts providing some after-sales-service by way of telling you where the next novice trials is to be held and how to go about entering it. There's more about riding in your first trial later in this book but for the moment we'll simply consider the very likely chance of you and Bill being annihilated. It's probably going to happen, so face it.

What you do next is obvious. You go home tail between your legs and lick your wounds. But, what else you do is to realise the difference between competitive sections and the fun things that you and the family have been using. You're not beaten, however. You've discovered that the learning business is going to start all over again — and all the fun with it. Your home-built sections get tougher and, as you improve, the family get more excited, scanning the motorcycle press for details of events to come and the results sheets to see who you topped — and who topped you last weekend.

Although I've concentrated on trials riding, it's nice to let off steam every now and again at a really fierce enduro. This shot dates back to 1965 and the Italian Valli Bergamasche.

The novice in his first trial should never be afraid to ask an expert his opinion on the way to tackle any given section. Between themselves experts play a lot of gamesmanship, trading false information in the hope it will give them an advantage over their fellow competitor. But 90 per cent of them remember the days when they were beginners and will happily pass on hints and tips to those who, although fellow riders, aren't in a position to endanger their chance of winning the trial.

Mind you, there are times to ask and times when your questions will be less than welcome. We've all seen an athlete making ready, for example, to try for a high-jump record. Just before his attempt he stands stationary, forcing his mind to empty of everything but the task in hand. He is schooling himself for absolute concentration and the whole world, other than the bar to be cleared, has ceased to exist.

Exactly the same is true of a superstar. It is part of his make up and one of the reasons why he has achieved success. As he gets a come-on from the observer telling him that it is his turn to try the section, he spends a few seconds stimulating himself mentally. This moment is not the one to ask him whether to use second or third gear for the climb. At best he will not hear you. At worst you may discover that at least one man has considerable doubts about your parentage!

As your ability improves you will find the desire to travel farther afield to higher-class events. Chances are that you will never compete in an international event or a round of the world championships, but you may well see such an event and your knowledge and degree of skill will make you appreciate, all the more, the prowess of the superstars.

Greatest of all women trials motorcyclists, Marjorie Cottle, took on the men, on level terms, in the 1930s, and regularly beat them. She's seen here on a sports model BSA Empire Star

I'm often asked why there are so few women competing in trials. My answer's no problem — I haven't the faintest idea.

There have, even from the early days, been a small, select band of females who have taken to, and performed brilliantly in what is, after all, a male-dominated sport. In the 1930s one or two women regularly beat the best men in the country. In more recent days, although some women have competed regularly, they have not had sufficient success to get amongst the top-award winners.

I see absolutely no reason why a woman, with the equal reflexes, tenacity and enthusiasm of a man, should not do just as well. The sole argument against a woman performing in trials is that she would not have the necessary strength to hold the bike steady in certain conditions. But, when you look at some of the less-than-Adonis males performing brilliantly in the toughest trials, that argument does not hold water.

I suspect that the real reason we have seen few women competitors stems from the reluctance of the male population to encourage their women-folk to take part. But, with women's liberation gaining strength every day, I shouldn't be surprised if the writing isn't already on the wall.

And it's not a bad thing either. I for one would be very glad to see a little more glamour and colour in the trials game. But it's going to take a few years and, male chauvinist that I am, I'll be glad that I'll have retired before a puce-pink-helmeted, mini-skirted college girl finishes higher in the results than I do.

Lady putting up a smoke screen is super-enthusiast Olga Kevelos -- a lass from Birmingham who, when she gave up active riding in the 1960s turned her hand to organising major events

Competitions Manager of the Auto-Cycle Union, Mary Driver was no mean performer on a trials bike in the 1960s. This shot shows her on a 250 cc Greeves machine

4
The machine

Although, almost from the birth of the industry, manufacturers have offered trials and other sports machines, the birth of today's sophisticated bike can be divided into the 1957 to '67 era and from '67 to today.

The '57 to '67 which I call the first decade of the modern trials machine, saw the death of the 350 cc and 500 cc four strokes, developed from roadsters, and the birth of the current lightweight.

During this period occurred the rise and fall of the great British factory teams. Royal Enfield, BSA, Ariel, Triumph and the AJS/Matchless combine put their faith in big-capacity machines and ran works teams with many riders employed full-time at the factory during the week.

The big, heavy machines took big men to ride and get the best out of them. That same decade saw the birth of the 250 cc two-stroke lightweight with Dot and Greeves leading the field with designs which eventually eclipsed the large-capacity bikes. But it was not an overnight affair.

For years I took my factory Greeves to big national trials. The great names of the time on their 350 and 500 cc bikes almost pitied me and I was definitely the odd man out. But I knew we were on the right track and that, eventually, the two-stroke engine would develop the wide spread of power so essential in trials. This, coupled with a lighter machine was to spell the death knell of the big bangers.

The last of the Greeves machines, the 250 cc Anglian was fantastically popular, its numbers dominating trials all over England. But it was basically a rehash of models which had gone before. Up until 1967 the Greeves was still a force to be reckoned with, winning the team award in the Scottish Six Days Trial. But the writing was on the wall. For two years earlier the first 250 cc Bultaco, developed by Sammy Miller, had made its appearance and was gradually eclipsing all other makes.

Greeves, unfortunately, did not rise to the challenge. What was needed was a completely new machine, the result of a design exercise started with a clean sheet of paper. However, the factory management didn't see it this way. After a few more years in the wilderness, Greeves, once the most respected competition firm in the business, gave up full-time motorcycle production and concentrated, instead, on their original products, invalid carriages.

When Bultaco's big rival Montesa saw the potential of the trials market and asked me to join them, I did not hesitate.

With the interest and rivalry of the Spanish factories, the modern trials machine went into its second phase. A third Barcelona factory got into the act with Mick Andrews designing an Ossa trials bike. The next few years were a virtual Spanish monopoly of the sport.

This lasted until 1972 when the Japanese came upon the scene. I signed to develop a machine for Kawasaki, then Mick Andrews went to Yamaha, Gordon Farley to Suzuki and Honda signed Sammy Miller after they had started work on a bike.

Perhaps the most famous trials bike ever made was the 500 cc Ariel specially developed by my great rival Sammy Miller. After Sammy relinquished GOV 132 for a job with the Bultaco factory I tested the old Ariel for the motorcycle press. The bike was great fun, but I didn't find a single section that a modern, light-weight two-fifty could not have conquered with considerably less rider effort

At the time of the Spanish invasion it looked as if the trials game was at last being considered seriously by big manufacturers. But when the Japanese came into the picture things really began to hum. Money was poured into development at a rate never known before and a full-scale programme of dealer and customer-involvement embarked upon. Top riders toured the world to demonstrate and give tuition.

From all this the modern-day trials machine has evolved.

Today's bike has highly-refined suspension with around seven inches of travel at the front, ground clearance has increased and the machine averages out at 40 lb lighter than the same capacity model of 10 years ago.

Also a lot of work has gone into ensuring trouble-free riding and the current competitor need know nothing about mechanics to enjoy his sport.

During the years, the trials bike has developed certain characteristics. These include a five-speed gearbox, chain tensioner, folding foot rests, 18 inch wheels at the rear and 21 inch at the front. More innovations are making themselves felt in the latest machines, including automatic oiling which does away with the need for mixing oil and fuel or having to use special petrol dispensers. On many machines you can now pull in the clutch and start the engine without having to find neutral.

Prices of all bikes have soared during the past few years but luckily the increasing popularity of the trials bike has ensured that the costs have not got out of all proportion as they seem to have done in other branches of the sport.

It's the old story of supply and demand. Minorities must pay out for their pleasures and only the soaring public interest in trials will keep the bike prices down.

To those who still consider that competition bikes are over-priced, and decide to do their own thing with a collection of tubes, an old engine and a set of welding bottles, I say just one thing. Don't.

The difficulties are enormous and take the resources of a factory design and development team, plus a lot of practical experience, to solve.

Consider just one point — how far apart the wheels should be. Sounds simple? It's not just a case of going out with a tape measure one dark night. Basically the longer the wheelbase the less likely it is that the front of the bike will rear up. The price to pay for that advantage is that rear wheel grip decreases as the wheels get further apart.

A short-wheelbase machine will concentrate more weight on the rear wheel when the throttle is tweaked but again, you get nothing for nothing in motorcycle design work, and the same set up will be liable to be very light at the front end.

Before someone shouts "compromise" at the top of their voice let me throw in another spanner. A bike fitted with an engine which has plenty of low-down power and therefore gives good grip, can get away with a fairly long wheelbase and, conversely, a bike with little bottom-end pull must have a shorter distance between the wheels.

Yes, that's right. It's all getting complicated and the back-yard mechanic who puts together a special may well finish up with a very workman-like machine. But the chances of it doing justice to his ability are remote. I'm a great believer in every man to his own job. When I want a wall built properly I call in a bricklayer and it's commonsense that when that same brickie wants a trials machine he should pick one that is the result of the work of experts.

I'm often asked what is my first principle when it comes to developing a trials bike. I start out to engineer the bike thinking all the time for the rawest novice. And, in that way, everyone benefits. The novice gets a machine that is easy to ride and the superstar has a bike that will allow him to display all his expertise.

One decision you will have to make when buying a machine is its capacity class. At the moment trials bikes — or machines calling themselves trials bikes — are available in sizes from 50 to 350 cc. At the present stage of engine development I do not think that anything under 125 cc has sufficient power to take on the type of sections likely to be found in a modern trial.

Bultaco, Montesa and Ossa all started with 250s, but then experimented with 350 cc and 125 cc-class machines.

In my opinion the 250 cc category is the ideal. I know far too many riders who have opted for a 125 because the initial sensation of its lighter weight makes the machine feel more manoeuvrable. Almost invariably they are quite happy for a couple of months and then they discover that they need the extra power delivered by the larger engine. And I consider that, at present, for all riders, barring the top-flight men, a 350 cc-class machine tends to be a little too fierce.

Whether you buy a new or secondhand machine will depend mainly on the finance you have available. There's no doubt that a new machine built by a reputable manufacturer, whose successes you can see detailed each week in the motorcycle press, will give you an advantage over most used mounts.

You will start off knowing that you have a good period in front of you without any likelihood of mechanical damage and repair-shop outlay. Of course, there are bargains to be had in the secondhand market and, ideally, you would like to know quite a lot of the bike's history before parting with your money. Strangely enough, a bike which has been used solely for trials and, therefore, properly maintained by an enthusiast could be a better bet than one which has been ridden continually down to the corner shop for the groceries and used as an everyday hack by the local scout troup.

Whatever capacity or make of machine — new or secondhand — you settle on, you will probably decide to do a few minor alterations before actually using it in an event. Thankfully, the days are gone when it is necessary to make drastic modifications to foot-rests, handlebar mountings and gear lever and brake pivot points. The current trials machine is a well thought-out and engineered device and really the only alterations necessary are for personal preferences such as the positioning of the handlebar levers and, perhaps, the sweep of the handlebars themselves.

This old TE model Greeves is 10 years out of date -- but it still provides its owner with an awful lot of fun

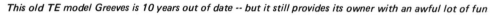

There are no hard and fast rules about control positioning except that you, the rider, should feel comfortable and at ease. Clutch and brake levers should fall naturally to hand and the bars should be wide enough to allow maximum leverage and feel, but not too wide so that on full lock one arm is over-extended.

Inevitably, whenever a new machine is put on the market the freelance development engineers get to work and bring out a large variety of special modifications. Some of these are worthwhile. Some are rubbish.

The secret here is to ask yourself why, if the mod is such a good idea, the manufacturer didn't fit it as original equipment. In some cases, where the answer is that to do so would have increased the price of the machine by a significant amount, it is quite conceivable that the mod could prove a useful asset to you.

But, beware of the tendency by some riders to alter their machines purely for the sake of adding the latest gimmick. An example of this is the current trend toward aluminium handlebars. A good quality alloy bar obviously reduces weight where it matters most — at the top of the machine. Manufacturers are in business to sell their bikes and therefore do not go overboard in adding exotic extras which would increase the price and make the product look less attractive. However, a cheaply made light-alloy bar, liable to snap at any moment, is obviously not such a good deal as the original steel version. Until all your 'get-offs' are planned ones — I would advise leaving the exotic goodies to the aces.

There are a wide variety of tyres available. And the choice can be quite bewildering. The British Auto-Cycle Union publishes a list of tyres which meet their specification and these are the only ones approved for British, Continental and International events. The regulations govern the sizes of the nobbles and the gaps between them and are designed to ensure that all riders have the same advantage.

These regulations have not been altered for many years, but great strides have been made in tyre design despite manufacturers having to stick to the same rigid specifications. The rubber mix of which the tyres are made has become much softer and has more gripping properties than the hard mix used before.

Nylon has replaced canvas as the carcass material allowing tyres to be built much lighter and, more important, with more supple side walls — essential for the caterpillar-like grip you will be trying to gain.

The production 250 Kawasaki. The fruit of my development work

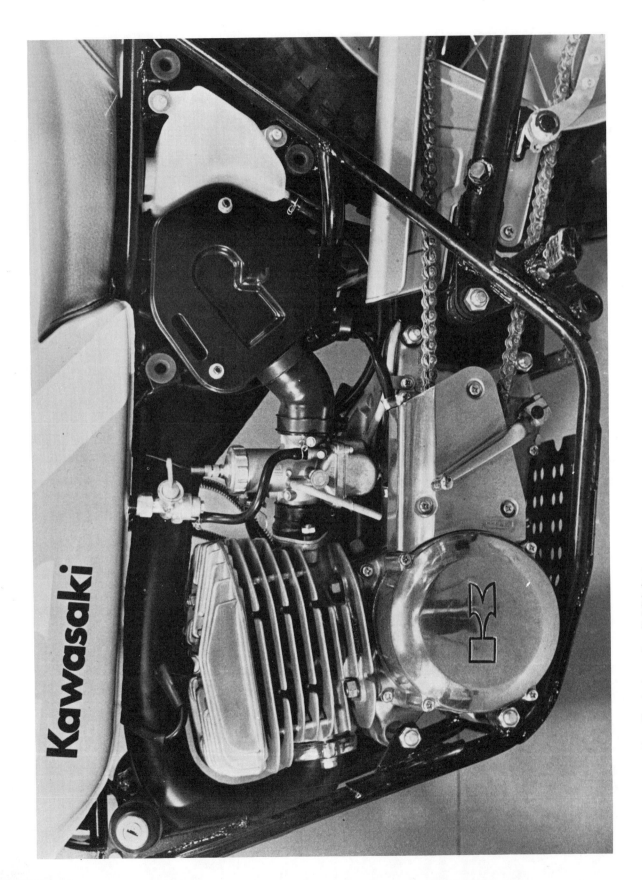

A very, very tidy machine. The air cleaner is well visible here

5
Clothing

Almost parallel with the great advancements made in the trials machine field during the past 15 years, is the way that riding clothing has improved.

Coats and suits

Back in the 1950s the ace on his big banger AJS, Ariel or BSA always wore a thick, over-length, heavy coat which, in theory, could be tucked between the legs and the fuel tank to keep the weather from reaching the knees. Such gear was clumsy, the sheer weight of the garment was a drag on the shoulders and the wrap-around skirt was a lot better in theory than in practice.

However, according to the wags of the time, the super-long gear had one advantage. The garments were christened 'footing coats' for the simple reason that if you did have to put a toe to the ground during an attempt on a section, you still got away with no penalty as the coat would mask your error. They weren't that long, of course, but they were pretty damn horrible.

When the footing coat became just too much to bear, we had the era of the two-piece, thornproof suit. Made principally by two manufacturers, they were originally available in a choice of colour — dark khaki or black — but later the drab grey-green was discontinued leaving only Mr Ford's favourite colour.

During the 1960s the thornproof with its waxed finish enjoyed a fashion vogue. Just about every trials rider in the world wore one, and British riders who competed overseas helped cover their expenses by smuggling over as many as could be fitted in a car boot.

In fact, behind the Iron Curtain, the suits were so highly regarded that it was not unusual for a Soviet rider to approach a West European at the end of a trial and ask to buy the suit off his back.

The main advantages of the waxed-cotton type suit are that they are hard wearing and more comfortable than the long coat. However, for trials work, they have quite a few disadvantages. In my opinion, they tend to let in water around the stitching and be heavy and stiff.

OK, so they look very smart when new, but after the first muddy trial they take on a very secondhand appearance and, no matter what you do, never look the same again — even after you have gone through the messy business of reproofing with warm wax or whatever.

The drab black colour also puts me off but, during the past few years, the suits have been available in a couple of colours but are still not what I would call bright.

This is a colourful sport that we enjoy and I see no reason why the rider should look as though he's just come from a very muddy funeral.

Thankfully, the 1970s heralded a complete new deal in trials clothing. I've two outfits and ring the changes depending on the weather. For sunny days — most of the time in California and every now and again in Britain — I use a one-piece nylon suit, light yet capable of providing the little protection necessary to avoid the odd graze in the event of a spill.

When the weather gets damp, I turn to my Vystram suit — a very supple, grain-finished

A flash-back to 1969 when my Montesa had large hubs and we carried air bottles to inflate the tyres. The next year's search for the lightness brought smaller hubs which decreased the unsprung weight considerably and we dispensed with the air bottles. Now, to inflate the tyres we use a small, high-pressure bicycle pump or just hope we don't hit trouble. The picture, taken at the Scottish Six Days Trial shows my overmits, which are worn on the road sections, tucked into my belt

plastic with one tremendous advantage. After an event, during the clean-the-bike session, the suit gets hosed down and scrubbed. And it comes up just like new. Both suits are finished in the green of my Kawasaki team, and let's face it, look smart.

Whether to go for a one-piece suit or separate jacket and trousers is purely a matter of personal preference. A two-piece set-up has the advantage of usually having a couple more pockets — got to keep the cigarettes somewhere! But it's a fallacy that you'll sweat more in one-piece gear. If you're going to sweat you'll do so whatever you are wearing.

Even the enthusiast in the sunniest parts of the world should remember that a graze can be painful and I always make a point of wearing, at least, a long-sleeved teeshirt on my top half. When doing so you can still stay with the trend, for most dealers now stock a range of shirts in very attractive designs. Clothing is essentially a protective thing but, luckily we are now, at least, getting some colourful gear.

Gloves

Although it is obvious that a beginner should wear a pair of light-weight gloves, the decision facing the professional rider is not so simple. Without gloves he may get chilly, his hands won't keep like a washing-up liquid advertisement but many aces think that's a small price to pay for the little extra degree of feel that can only come from bare hands. Anyway the superstar isn't likely to step off the bike quite so often and risk a barked knuckle.

I compromise, wearing light leather gloves between sections and stuffing them into a pocket when the time comes to attack a section.

Another tip, very useful on trials like the Scottish Six Days, is to have a pair of oil-skin overmits to wear on long stretches between sections. At the hazards they can be looped into the belt.

Some hard men scorn the use of gloves at all times but then have to spend 10 minutes at each section with their hands an inch from the cylinder head trying to get some feeling back into their fingers.

*Here I am wearing my two-piece riding
suit and rubber boots. I don't wear
gloves here*

*Supreme concentration - I am wearing
all the right clothing - note my motocross boots and one piece suit*

Boots

Again we are faced with a choice of two different types, each having its own advantages. Maybe I'm a bit of a snob but I rather go for leather footwear. I appreciate that a pair of the real thing can be very expensive but the support a good pair of boots gives pays dividends. I also believe that the relatively close fit of a proper boot increases pedal sensitivity.

The alternative is rubber wellingtons. Now let's get one thing straight. I'm talking about industrial boots not the corner-shop specials that you use to walk the dog in the forest, go fishing, or clean the snow from the front porch. Industrial wellington boots have steel toe caps and heavy reinforced rubber paddings to protect the shins and ankles. Do wear decent boots; shoes or ordinary boots may be cheaper but try it and you could be doing wheelchair trials for a week or two. With the right gear you'd be very unlucky to even sprain an ankle.

Head wear

In England there's been a lot of controversy over helmet compulsion for road use, but I've made up my mind that, even if we are talking about the chances of a one-in-a-million accident, a helmet must be worth wearing and now I rarely go without.

I guess I've tried just about every helmet on the market before finding one that really suited me. But now that I have, I see it as part of my full trials rigout.

That's snow in the background and me in the foreground not about to rob a bank but with a leather face mask which is the ideal extra when the weather gets tough

A good quality 'space' helmet - without the visor for trials riding

Goggles

Back in the dark days when I started riding trials, no competitor worth his salt would be seen out without a pair of goggles. Some used the heavy, leather-framed RAF pattern with laminated glass lenses. Others settled for simple one-piece plastic spectacles.

However, nowadays the goggle has all-but disappeared from the trials scene, especially in the superstar type of event. I believe the reason is the recent trend towards wearing helmets in events. These helmets can all be fitted with peaks which shield the riders' eyes from most of the debris which can be flung up from the front wheel. The goggle, therefore, is not necessary except in long-distance events such as the Scottish Six Days Trial, where considerable road-work is necessary.

I've just thought of another reason why we used to wear goggles. In the pre-crash helmet era most riders wore flat caps. And these wouldn't stay on unless there was a goggles strap around them.

The helmet peak also serves to keep the sun out of the eyes on steep climbs etc. I would advise, however, 'straight out' type peaks as opposed to the 'downward slope' models which can restrict vision when tackling the sections.

Caring for the gear

Good trials clothing can be expensive and, therefore, it makes good sense to delay renewal as long as possible by keeping it in decent condition.

I've already dealt with scrubbing off Vystram-type suits. The same thing should not be done with the thornproof variety as this will simply remove the wax-coating, converting something which was fairly waterproof into little better than blotting paper.

Thornproof suits should be gently sprayed down and left to dry slowly.

Boots come in for the same go-slowly treatment. Leather should be treated with leather 'food' and left to dry out slowly in, at most, a warm room. Many's the pair of week's wages that have been completely destroyed by an hour's forced drying in front of a roaring fire or a radiator.

When at last dry, by the approved method, boots should be treated to dubbin or polish. Neatsfoot oil is a natural leather food processed from cows' hooves and helps keep the material supple as well as water resistant.

If a helmet gets really wet inside, it too, should be allowed to dry with no application of heat. Never hang a helmet by its harness and don't throw it in the boot of the car with the tool box and spare wheel. A helmet should have its own bag to protect it. Scratches and abrasions can destroy the top coating, and allow the weather in, reducing the effectiveness of the hat in the event of a fall.

6
Transporting the beast

Although trials bikes should be 100 per cent legal for use on the public roads, it's obvious that a form of transporting the machine for long distances is necessary.

There are, basically, five different methods of transporting the bike so we'll deal with them one at a time.

The pick-up truck

It's convenient, can carry three or even four bikes with ease, but you are considerably restricted as the cab often will not accommodate the average family in comfort. And there's no point in a day's fun if it means an hour or two's agony at either end.

If you do decide to go the pick-up route, it's worth making an effort to get the bikes sitting securely in the back. The ideal is to build a metal rack into which the wheels will lodge.

Even the smallest pick-up — this one is a BLMC Mini, can be used for getting the bike to and from meetings

The van

This is a good deal for a group of three or four lads touring around competing in trials. With a van the bikes stay out of the weather, you have got somewhere to change and expenses can be split up among the passengers. But vans with bikes in them tend to get messy. It's often not possible to rid the bike of mud before loading up and when you get home, you'll be faced with the job of cleaning the van as well as the bike.

A van has its advantages and that plank will make the on- and off-loading considerably easier

The trailer

I use an open trailer if needing to transport three bikes but I wish I didn't have to. Another vehicle hanging on behind the car is a thing I would rather not have to worry about. A trailer certainly cancels out many of the disadvantages of a pick-up and a van but there are added aggravations with reversing, parking, speed limits and maintenance.

If you do decide to use a trailer, make sure that the unit is up to the job. When I had my trailer built I specified the best wheels, suspension units, tyres and brakes that money could buy. Certainly, I was worried about the safety of the bikes but also for other road users. A runaway trailer is a dangerous thing.

Trailers come in all shapes and sizes. This one was custom-built for two bikes

Across the back of the car

The modern trials bike is so light and slim that it can be easily carried on a frame across the back of a car. I used this system of transporting a machine for many years with no trouble but, even this, seemingly ideal, method has its drawbacks.

With a narrow car the bike's wheels will overhang which is something to be constantly borne in mind when driving in towns or parking in confined spaces. It's possible that the car's rear lights will be obscured and, with some vehicles, access to the boot will be difficult. Also you can carry only one machine.

The system's main advantage is that you are still driving a car with no hassle over special trailer speed limits and, for the traveller who uses ferries, the saving in not having to pay for trailer space can be considerable.

No van, no rack, no pick-up? All this lad has in the way of transport is a car -- and a pretty small car at that. But where there's a will there's a way -- even if it means leaving the boot lid at home

Up and on the car

Now for the best toy I've ever owned. It's a rack that enables two or three machines to be carried on the rear of the car with all the advantages of the system mentioned previously, but none of the drawbacks.

With the machines sitting over the car boot (trunk) and their front wheels just short of the rear window, we've got a transportation set-up which has no side overhang and, if correctly sited, does not obscure the rear lights or vision through the rear window.

The rack on my car is fitted with just three quick-release pins. Access to the boot is easy. I simply pull two of the pins and the whole assembly, bikes and all, swings back with next to no effort.

I guess I've tried just about every method of transporting a bike — including an ill-fated session with a one-wheel trailer that wouldn't reverse, and I reckon that running the bikes up the back of the car is the only real answer. It's possible I'm wrong but, until we develop a bike that will fold up and fit into an automobile's glove compartment, I'll stick with what I've got.

My current method of transporting my trials machinery -- and the greatest toy I have ever had

7
Self preparation

No, don't worry, I'm not going to embark on a series of pages on how 20-mile walks, weightlifting and a life in which the most exciting happenings are meals of raw carrots and beetroot juice, is necessary to turn you into a passable trials rider.

To tell the truth, I smoke too many cigarettes, like a drink, a good time, and my only consideration of a 20-mile trip is how much fuel the car will use.

But then I'm a naturally healthy person with no weight problem — and that fact I put down to riding bikes ever since I was 15.

The way I see it is that every person needs some form of physical exercise and, if you get it doing something you really enjoy, you've got to be on a winner every way.

A guy who is naturally non-athletic will baulk at long sessions of road work. I've seen people convinced that they need some exercise. They embark on an ambitious programme of exercises that make an army assault course look like a Sunday morning walk-the-dog stroll in the park. That's fine except that the next three days are spent in bed recovering and they're back to square one.

When an enthusiast starts out riding a trials bike he naturally takes things easy as he is limited by, if nothing else, his ability. After a fairly short session, his arms and legs tell him that he has done enough for the day. And, if he doesn't heed nature's warning system, he'll find out the next morning.

But even so, he'll know the cause of each little muscular twinge and as he builds up the length of each practice session, the twinges get less as the enjoyment and experience increase. With more and more riding he'll find that he can cope with increasing exercise which tunes in his whole body. Soon he'll be putting in a day's riding exercise which would put good neighbour Bill on his back in the recovery ward for a week.

But what you are expecting out of this chapter is a little down-to-earth advice, so I'll split up trials riders into five groups and we'll look at the physical requirements of each in turn.

The family funster

This man is going to get all the exercise he needs out of his sport and, unless he intends to go into the game seriously, riding the bike is all he needs to keep physically fit.

Let's face it, everyone likes to be fit — it's the sweat involved with long physical work-outs, depressing and anti-social diet that turns most people off.

What trials offer is an easy, fun way to keep yourself in trim. The over-weight man will get back to the stage of enjoying seeing a weighing machine instead of hastening past with a flash of guilt.

Physical endurance increases fantastically. In my two-year lay-off after I left Montesa I could feel myself almost going to seed. Back riding again, I'm getting fitter every day and feeling better mentally for it as well. Trials is no Charles Atlas course — simply a way of having a good time which also keeps the body in fine tune. And that can't be bad.

The youngster

He's 13 years old and up and so damn tough that he's going to take all the little knocks and aches that even a raw novice on a super rough day out can absorb, without even flinching. And, even if he does over-reach himself a little, the surplus of determination that exists with youth will see him through. Not for our teenager the restrictive and boring series of press-ups. He's got so much energy that he needs the bike to get some of it out of his system.

The would-be pro

Here we're getting a little bit serious for this man's got his eye on a career on two wheels but, bearing in mind that he still hasn't got the necessary ability to throw up his regular job, I'm still not going to advocate a programme of physical training.

This man needs to improve his riding, to bring his reactions to the fine pitch needed for big-time competition. And, if he's serious, that means riding, and still more riding, at every available opportunity. Obviously, such a lot of work out in the field is going to keep him just as fit as he needs to be.

The pro

All right, now we are in the big time. If our man is going to eat and his family are going to get jam on their bread, he's got to be a winner.

He's looking for superstar status. He wants the press acclaims, the world travel and the large cash awards that go to the winners in our sport. And, to some extent, he's got to pay for it with a serious programme of running, press-ups, etc. It may sound like a drag, but what that man is building up is a fantastic amount of self-confidence that pays off when the chips are down.

I've been through an army paratrooper course and still do some cross-country running. I know exactly my physical limitations and the thought of a long, tough trial holds no worries for me now.

I remember a superstar who let himself go to seed. In his day he was up among the best but he got complacent, deciding his natural ability was so great that his body could get along without any discipline. It got to the state where the prospect of walking up a long section to inspect its various difficulties was just too much effort. Instead, he would sit at the bottom and quiz the other men who had returned from the climb. That was OK for a time but his competitors very soon caught on that they were being taken for mugs. The lads got together and decided on a plan of campaign.

As each returned from one particular section in a very important trial they assured the star that he needed to be going as quickly as possible at the brow of the hill so as to be able to plough through a sea of thick mud on the other side.

When the ace arrived at the top, flat out in third gear, he sailed over, couldn't turn sharp right as the markers demanded and sailed straight into a 10 feet deep lake of stagnant, smelly water. The rest of the competitors pulled him and his bike out.

Now he's learnt a lesson and is back training with the rest.

The old pro

This chap's had his day near the top of the tree and now he's back riding for fun again. And we've gone full circle for his physical requirements are just the same as before he hit the pro route. Now he wants to keep looking and feeling young and rather than a dull, weekly work-out at Joe's gym, he's out on his trials bike each weekend, probably with his kids. He's had a good life with trials but knows it's not all over yet.

Diet

I'm fortunate in that, when riding in trials I weigh a near constant 147 lb whatever I eat or drink and, therefore, I never need any form of special diet. I am eternally grateful that I can eat anything but I put this down to trials riding keeping me fit and constitutionally healthy.

When business forces a lay-off from competition for a spell, I do put on a little weight — and in the wrong places.

From this, and the experience of others, I believe that any normal overweight problem can probably be overcome by trials riding and I know women who are adamant that their trim figures owe more to bike work than to complicated diets and special exercises.

Smoking

It's going to be a little difficult here to come out against smoking as I feel I should. I've never been one for the 'don't do as I do, do as I tell you' school. All I can really say is that I'm sure they don't do me any good, and I'd advise anyone not to start smoking.

On one hand I've no evidence to suggest that tobacco has done me any harm. On the other, and much more important this, perhaps if I didn't smoke there would be five instead of three world-title cups in my trophy cabinet.

Drink

Well, I booze as well, but very little. I can see no special point in abstaining totally but, conversely, too much liquor the night before, and a hang-over during the trial, is certainly not on. (Although there is a Yorkshire school of thought which says booze cures pre-event nerves!) To the man who puts a lot of beer away the night before, I'll simply ask this — can a fat tum flapping around in the middle of a section help balance?

Women

Let's get one thing straight. We're talking about the advisability of spending the night with the wife, girlfriend or whatever on the eve of an important trial.

Next to a trials bike, women must be the most beautiful thing God ever created and I love 'em all.

Face it, the trials star, travelling away from home, with the glamour of a competition in a virile sport and with cash in his pocket need never be short of female company.

Company and perhaps the release of a few pre-trial tensions — that's a nice way of putting it — can be quite understandable. But an all-night session with just a couple of hours' exhausted sleep between 6 and 8 am isn't the perfect start to an important event.

Also any guilt feelings that might exist aren't going to help a man's performance in the trial.

Some riders seem to feel that they can get away with no sleep and still do well the next day.

And, even during the toughest trial of the lot, the Scottish Six Days, some riders are, to put it bluntly, irresponsible. I remember one occasion when a works rider picked up a girl and finished up with her in the back of his car on the loch-side just out of town. The pair were doing the moon-bathing bit when the local police arrived. A torch was shone onto the rear seat. Before the policeman could finish the 'what's all this 'ere' line, the rider had leapt, still naked, into the front of the car, started the engine and was off. The police car gave chase and it took 20 minutes hectic driving before the law gave up the race.

All very funny in retrospect but just imagine the state of mind of the man the next morning. He was certain the police had got his number and that he faced charges of disturbing the peace, indecent exposure, lewd exhibitionism, a dozen different traffic offences from the chase and the prospect of trying to explain the whole deal to his wife later. During the next day's ride he could not have had his mind completely on the job in hand.

Similar problems must have faced the man who crept out of a woman's flat at 6 am to get to the start of the trial and saw, as he passed the hall stand, the dim outline of her husband's hat — a policeman's helmet!

Let's sum it all up like this. If you can stand the odd five-mile walk before a trial, all well and good, but remember that the superstar should have a sense of priority and responsibility to himself, his factory, and to his bank balance.

Richard Sunter, on the works bike, during the British round of the World Trials Championship, Rhayader, March 1974

Nigel Birkett and myself have just signed a 'Works' contract

8
One job in seven

The question most asked of any factory rider is, perhaps not surprisingly, not how he tackles any given section but how he got to be where he is. How he turns a hobby into a paying game? And how he manages to earn his bread just by doing what he likes best.

The question has been asked me many a time and is really best answered by relating just how I came to be doing the job I have today.

There are seven major factories interested in trials, four in Japan and three in Spain. Each of them has a development engineer. It's a very sobering thought that of the world's population only seven jobs are available — and I've been fortunate enough to have my share of them.

It all started when I was 13 years old when I began making a nuisance of myself at the motorcycle shop and welding business of an enthusiast in East London. All my out-of-school time was spent plaguing the owner for a chance to clean the bikes or help with the welding. The result of this was that even before I left school — a grammar school with the emphasis on academic virtues rather than the practical ones, I was able to weld proficiently with gas or electric arc and had learned a lot about the stresses and strains of metal fabrications.

The part time job at the motorcycle and general engineers put me in touch with every facet of the sport. We built speedway, grasstrack, trials and scrambles specials and I helped on every one of them. Not only that, but I saw the mistakes that were made and gloried in the successes achieved. All this background helped me get a job as maintenance welder at Stanstead airport, an unheard of responsibility for a 17-year-old.

Since my 16th birthday I was riding regularly and did quite a lot of local scrambling before being called up for national service.

The transition from well-paid welding to 85p a week private was a disaster. Up until the time I put on uniform I had spent all my spare time on bikes and suddenly I didn't have the money to fill their tanks with petrol, let alone maintain them.

Then along came my first fairy godfather in the shape of a local motorcycle dealer who saw the problem I was up against. He had watched me ride before call-up and decided to provide me with bikes to continue my competition career. He bought BSA Gold Star and Triumph scramblers. It was at this time that the small Essex company of Invacar — makers of invalid carriages, decided to launch out into the trials market. And in 1957 produced their first Greeves production model, designed by the great Brian Stonebridge.

My sponsor bought the first model off the production line and when I arrived home from the army one Saturday he showed it to me and announced I was to ride it the next day.

In a trial which favoured early numbers, my last minute entry had me riding number 302. That I was able to finish third showed just what sort of an impact that early Greeves had.

My confidence was also being boosted at this time in another direction. With me in the army were big-name works riders including Jeff Smith, Pat Britain, Peter Stirland, Eric Adcock, and Bill Brooker — later to become my competition manager at Greeves.

We all rode trials for the army on identical Matchless G3L 350 cc machines. The fact that

Scrambling days -- on a 500cc Triumph-engined BSA that I built and used in the late fifties.

I've even tried scrambling, with some success, on a 250cc Greeves outfit

I spent quite some time riding professional speedway but this shot shows me using a 360cc Greeves-engined bike during the time I was experimenting with two-strokes on the shale

I managed to win more trials than I lost really gave me heart.

I've just said that the Matchlesses were standard, but that's a little far from the truth. Being on the trials scene I had little else to do but spend each weekday working on the machine. One afternoon, wanting a little more power, I set to work surreptitiously to fit a scrambles camshaft. The timing chest was not big enough to accommodate the big cam and I had to set about delicately enlarging it with a cold chisel. This was less than successful as I cut straight through into the big end feedline. Sweating that I would be found out, I bodged things up with plastic metal. The Heath Robinson repair lasted out my service days and was still on the bike when I left.

Come to think of it, the only standard thing about our bikes was the khaki paint, but somehow always passed the technical inspection!

At last my two years' involuntary service were up, and I was offered my old job back at Stanstead airport. My dealer friend who had provided my scrambles bikes also offered me a job and after the way he had helped me I couldn't say no.

Under his banner I continued to ride Greeves machines until 1960 when two big things happened at once for me. I was offered full factory support by Greeves who had been impressed by my record; and a local businessman offered me the money to start my own shop.

Brian Stonebridge who acted as development engineer for Greeves, was killed in a road accident and the post was never, really, filled again. Instead the task was handled by the design staff, the competition manager and the team of works riders.

I gradually worked my way up to become the factory's top trials man but the exhilaration of this was always dampened by the fact that the company did not seem interested in producing a new bike or even letting me do so for them. As early as 1962 Dot brought out what was then an advanced machine and, to my mind, the writing was on the wall for Greeves, who were on a steady downhill track.

I eventually went to the directors and told them that the bike that had lasted them for the last eight years was too long in the tooth and that a new model was needed.

There was no reason why the plan should not have been put into action. Although a small company, Greeves had all the workshop facilities including a foundry and at one stage I was actually given the go ahead to build my idea of a superbike.

Then, at the last moment, the whole deal was called off because one director did not have the confidence that there was a market for the machine. A short while later Bultaco headed the Spanish invasion of the trials game with what was to be a real money spinner. We could have had an equally good, or even better, bike with a British label on the tank. The refusal to see the scope of the market was the final straw for me. And I gave in my notice.

I bought myself a Bultaco and rode it privately in 10 events. I got seven firsts, one second and a third place. This and the fact that the press made it clear that I was not allied to any factory, probably influenced Montesa who asked me to look at a new off-road bike that they wanted to put into production.

Unknown to them, a Dutchman, Henk Vink, the Montesa concessionaire for Holland, had been playing with a modified machine for a few months and I had already tried this on the Continent and so had a fair idea what to expect.

On my way to see the British agent I decided that, although I could ride the bike and give an immediate assessment of its performance and potential, to do so with no contract or recompense would, in fact, be giving away the benefit of my 15 years' experience. It may sound a little commercial but when I arrived my mind was made up. No fee — no opinion.

I tried the bike over some local land and, when I had finished, the importer asked me what I thought. I made a few general comments but before I had even finished the first sentence he'd sent his son rushing to the house for a pen and paper.

I told him he just had to be kidding, and that, until we had discussed terms, I wasn't coming across with any more information.

Montesa days. The gent on the right, in the equally snappy headgear, is the Spanish factory's competition manager, Alberto Mallofre

A shot from my days as an instructor at a speedway school run at the East London Hackney Stadium. Riders from all branches of the sport tried their hands at the school. I'm shown here with road racers Barry Sheene on my right, and Dave Potter

The outcome of this was a series of visits to the Montesa factory at Barcelona during which I inspected their resources and current range of machines and said that I could see no reason why we could not produce the best trials bike in the world.

Again I ran into management problems. Half of the company's directors were eager to go, but the other half were very diffident as Bultaco were ruling the roost with their own machine on which Sammy Miller had just won the European championship. I finally managed to convince the company that I could better the Bultaco but because of the boardroom split I had to settle for peanut wages.

I took the job and the peanuts, regarding it simply as a stepping stone to greater things to come.

And the bike was a winner. In 1969, on the first prototype, I took the European championship but only after an awful lot of sweat during which time I almost made an enemy.

The Montesa competition manager Pedro Pi seemed to resent my appearance on the scene and things were very cool between us. I got the impression he didn't understand why the company needed to import a foreigner to build a trials machine. The fact of the matter is that Pedro had spent two years working on a similar project and was still not far advanced from the prototypes I'd tried in Holland and England. I wanted to be associated with a real winner and was ready to go flat out for it and was so determined myself that I couldn't have been the easiest person to get along with.

Things got more and more difficult and soon the whole future of our being able to work together began to evolve around one particular test section just outside Barcelona. The section which Pedro had long deemed impossible was an enormous rock step with a drop so steep on one side that, if you went over, your clothes would be out of fashion by the time you hit the bottom.

With a team of catchers at the ready I experimented with every possible form of front fork angle, rear suspension settings, wheelbase and engine characteristic until, one day, the step was conquered. Pedro, too, found that on the finished bike he was able to do the impossible and I think that at that moment accepted me and my ideas.

Now we are the greatest of friends and even though I work for Kawasaki, the Spaniard turns the full facilities of Montesa over to me every time I am in Barcelona.

The Montesa was a fantastic success story, winning the team award in the Scottish Six Days Trial in 1969 to '72 inclusive, plus the 1969 European championship, national titles in Holland, France, Spain and Finland and three industrial design awards. And with minimal improvements, the model is still the same force to be reckoned with today.

The results could hardly have been better for the doubting Montesa directors but, having built the bike, I then got the impression that I was no longer wanted. They had a good bike on the production line but even so were unable to see the potential of the trials market as I've always done.

The trophies don't always stay in the loft. I had to get all 700 down and clean them for this publicity shot taken during my Montesa days

Again I had to summon up courage and burn my boats behind me. Because of my all-devouring interest in riding bikes I had had to give up my shop and the Smith fortunes were at their lowest ebb yet. But already I was looking to Japan. Years before, I had written to Kawasaki telling them of the world-wide trials market that was sure to open up but received a reply saying that they were not ready for that sort of expansion at that time.

When I decided to leave Montesa in 1970 I was aware that I had built the best trials bike that yet existed. But I did not feel that the Spaniards were taking trials to the people.

I see a future in which my branch of the sport is five times bigger than all other forms of motorcycle competitions combined. All the Japanese factories can now see this potential and I only hope they believe in it as fervently as I do.

With Montesa settling back on their laurels, I was faced with the need to break my contract. I could not stand another 10 years frustration as I experienced with Greeves and could not bear the feeling that I was simply a Montesa possession. I decided that the way to break my contract was to ride another machine. And, faced with an ethical problem of not wishing to give publicity to another factory, I built my own bike which I named The Stag.

I was free again, but this time my independent attitude misfired. Quitting Montesa before I had another job nearly put me on the breadline. I was almost standing on the white cliffs of Dover looking for the Japanese to beckon — and they did take their time. It was not until May 1972 that I signed with Kawasaki and became the first foreign development engineer to be employed by a Japanese company.

Even then I did not pressure them. I had been corresponding with Yamaha and we had got to the stage of discussing terms but then came a call from Henk Vink who was by then the Benelux importer of Kawasaki. He told me that he had recommended me and, following a call from Japan, I met Kawasaki's representative in London and eventually signed a contract.

At the time I joined Kawasaki, trials machines, which had nearly all been of 250 cc, were branching out into larger capacities. Bultaco were developing a 325 cc and there were rumours that Ossa, too, were going the big-bike route. I therefore advised that we at Kawasaki investigate the large-capacity area, basing the first prototype on a 450 cc engine that the factory had just designed for motocross.

Although the 450 didn't lead to a production bike it did give my Japanese team some experience and knowledge of the trials game. Up until that time they only had one thing going for them — enthusiasm.

My first job was to build a prototype trials bike around the 450 and take that and some Spanish machines to the factory to show them just what trials machines were all about. The factory saw the 450 prototype in October 1972 and by the following May they had built three replicas for us to use in the Scottish Six Days Trial.

The bikes were far from perfect, especially as they arrived in England just three days before the event and I had very little time to do finishing touches. However, all three got through the marathon event and we won the 500 cc cup. The 450 served to educate the Japanese engineers into the peculiarities of trials machines. Sure, mistakes were made, but that's really the best way to learn.

Two months later a new 250 cc engine came along and with it we were able to build a much more viable machine. My works rider, Richard Sunter, and I were getting into the awards regularly. The 250 enabled me to put a lot of theories into practice. The best way for a motor-cycle development engineer to work is to assume that the buyer will have little natural ability and therefore must depend upon the bike to do a great deal. Some engineers have so much riding ability that they could win a trial riding a lawn mower. Unfortunately, sometimes this results in their building lawn mowers.

Not that the first 250 was perfect. The engine had fantastic bottom end power but this simply disappeared as the revs got higher and although it was possible to win a trial on the bike, it wasn't the greatest fun to ride on the road.

With some trepidation I instructed the engineers in Japan to give me more top-end power.

The reason I was worried was that, in motorcycle engineering, you get nothing for nothing. And I was scared that our increase on top-end power would be at the sacrifice of low-down torque.

When I went to Japan in November 1973 to see the outcome of their work I was a little apprehensive as I climbed on the machine. But the lads had really delivered the goods. There was power at the top and, somehow, it was all still there in the lower rev band.

When I worked with Greeves I lived just half an hour by road away from the factory. With Montesa I was three hours off by plane. But Kawasaki is a full day's journey by jet. And it's only the modern technological advances that make it possible for a development engineer to be so remote from its company's headquarters.

With Greeves we had incessant, recurring, troubles. Flywheel bosses would shear and the main bearings fitted in them would not really have done service on a roller skate. A modern trials bike is now so trouble-free that such problems are things of the past.

With Kawasaki, unlike some other factories, we did not rush out to sign a superstar from another company. Instead, the company showed sufficient confidence in me to allow me to go out talent-spotting and contract a rider who had yet to make the big time. I picked Richard Sunter as a man who will one day be in the superstar bracket. I first noticed him when I was riding for Montesa when he was just starting in the game. It was clear to me then that one day he would be able to beat me and I was glad I was able to give him his chance.

Once Richard had to prepare his own machinery. Now he travels the world, goes to Disney Land, sunbathes in California and skis in Bavaria.

But there's a debit side too for a youngster. His position in a team must depend on results. And those same results will depend solely on his determination to reach the top. At times he may feel anguish at not doing well but, rather than retreat into a sea of self pity, he must re-double his aggression and determination to improve.

That same strain can affect the big-time pro. Trials have only one winner and if a rider's turn doesn't come around often enough it is a heavy load for him to bear.

Factories normally run more than one rider and big-time companies are fickle over superstars. If one man does not hit the headlines too often he may well find he is getting the cold shoulder from his employers.

So it's not all milk and honey for the superstars. Some get to the top the hard way, others almost have a works ride handed to them on a plate. Regardless of the route they used, once they're at the top the big struggle is to stay there. This is a problem that will cause consternation to perhaps only one in a thousand reading this. So I'll get to your problem and help you.

Components of the production 250 Kawasaki. Note the brake shoe condition indicator, the protected cables and the chain oiler

9

Riding the hazards

Let's get one thing straight from the start. Sections can be failed and marks lost before a rider even makes his attempt. What that apparent nonsense really means is that a brilliant attempt at a hazard by a top-class rider can result in a disaster unless the man has done his homework first. And that homework starts the minute he gets to the section and begins his inspection.

Even if you're the most inexperienced novice, don't ever be scared of spending as much time as you need to explore all the problems that a section has to offer. We've all seen the golfer lining up for what looks like such an easy shot that a five-year-old could sink with a tennis racket. He's not playing to the crowd but making sure that he knows the lie of the land perfectly and that he's got everything working for him when he makes the play that could earn or lose him the match and those thousands of dollars.

With the bike parked we're ready to do a little leg work. And I don't care if you were born, raised, went to school, met your first girlfriend and now work not 100 yards from the hazard — if you want to succeed, go over every inch of the problem.

Before we get onto specific types of sections let me lay down one cardinal rule. Whenever possible, ride over everything as opposed to trying to go round obstacles. A double turn just to avoid a rock or tree stump will invariably lead to more aggravation than by attacking square on. It's all a matter of having confidence in your own ability. There's a way to develop this, which initially, may sound a little frightening but it really works. All you need is a 12 inch diameter log, a couple of bricks, and a small helping of nerve.

What you're going to do is to ride your bike over the log. With the log chocked with the bricks, approach it in second gear with the engine pulling steadily. Just before reaching the log, roll off the throttle to depress the front forks, steadily open it again and pull gently and squarely back on the bars. The combination of the front fork elongating, the drive from the engine and the lift on the bars will raise the front wheel cleanly up and over the log. At this point your weight should be thrown forward to help the back wheel rise and follow its mate to the other side.

The expert still carries out this form of practice although he uses a 40 gallon oil drum — and that's pretty high. You can slowly graduate from the small log to larger obstacles, gaining confidence all the time. And when you reach the oil drum level of expertise, the time will come when the bike gets stuck on its crankcase, high on the drum. You would give anything to be able to put a foot down and steady the plot but there's just no way your leg is going to make that long a trip.

So now we're learning two things — how to climb over obstacles and, just as important, building up confidence and resistance against putting a foot down.

When you've got this little exercise off pat we can make the whole deal a lot more difficult by simply removing those bricks. Now that nice static log has turned live, and resembles a rock which could move under you in a second. As you practice, and become

It is possible, on level ground, to have both wheels off the ground at once! It's not easy, just possible. It's part of learning to clear obstacles such as felled trees. Start with a beer can laid on its side. The object is to ride over it without marking it. Could be you'll need quite a few empty ones!
Approach the can slowly. Depress the forks and, as they rise again, gently pull on the bars and open the throttle. The front wheel is now in the air. Determine the point, then change your body position and thrust forward on the bars. The effect of this sudden change is to lift the rear wheel, almost as if there were a pivot under the crankcase. It'll take a while to master

Now we can increase the size of the can slightly. This is a 40-gallon oil drum, but exactly the same technique will bring the same success. In this shot I have cleared the front wheel and the crankcase over the can and am ready to transfer my weight to the front

Weight is now going to the fore and the back wheel is trying to climb the drum. Note that the crankcase has not crashed down

Hey presto. Success. I'm over but just look at those arms. Ideally they should be locked straight at the elbows. I got away with it but a little more angle on the front wheel and I would have been off on my ear. Unless you are a real ace don't try this with an empty drum, whether it is chocked or not, - or there'll be bikes, bodies and barrels flying in all directions!

You are unlikely to find oil drums lurking in the woods - and unlikely to find sections built of tree trunks quite this high - but photographer Graham Forsdyke discovered this beauty and challenged me to climb it. Exactly the same procedure as with the oil drum. Front wheel high enough to clear the obstacle and not bounce me back off it.

We're well and truly on the log and it's an awful long way down

Looking good. On the way down ready to brace my arms

Another success, (providing he did'nt spot the dab on the blind side) and this time the front wheel is staying

more and more proficient, not only will you find that what was, initially, scary has become quite good fun but that you are, unconsciously, wanting less and less to have that steadying prod.

Right, so now we're full of confidence and ready to attack the section. Hold it. Have we made a friend of the observer yet? No, I'm not being cynical. The observer is the man or woman who is standing in the pouring rain so that you can have a day's sport. He's also the one who is going to decide your score on that particular section and, whilst I'm not suggesting that you go in with a bribe, a friendly smile and a how-do isn't going to do your chances any harm if it comes to the benefit of any doubt.

Whilst we're giving the observer the big hello, it is the time to check any doubts you may have on the section. In Ireland, observers tend to be pretty tough and will dock you five marks for even brushing up against a marker, while in England most officials will let you do practically anything short of knocking it over before they debit your score. A quiet word will ascertain just what his views are. The same thing goes for sections which are marked with tape. With the loose tape its quite possible to widen the arc on a corner by running so close to the tape that you actually move it outwards with your arm. Again some observers see this as quite a permissible manoeuvre, whilst others automatically mark down a five.

At this time you may also have to make a big decision. It's quite possible that in walking the section you have found a line, unused by any other competitor, that you feel would give you an advantage. Some, usually inexperienced, observers may see you take a completely different approach to the problem and dock you five purely for that reason. Therefore, it is perhaps a good idea to chat to the official first, tell him of your intention, and ask him to confirm that it is within the spirit of the regulations. And here the trouble can start, because it is quite conceivable that, just because you have brought up a different line, he will automatically consider it wrong. My only advice here, is if you are in real doubt, you must have a quiet word — and I do mean quiet for there's no point in telling everyone else of your good idea.

However, if you are 100 per cent sure of your facts and that your line in the section could be argued out afterwards as being legal, I advise you to get on with it, speak to no one. To do so with a dogmatic observer could cost you the opportunity of the only clean on that hazard. Got the message? Be your own psychologist and play it all by ear.

First thing that will come to mind is the obvious line through the section, either because it avoids any of the problem spots or because, during your time there, you see a dozen or so other riders use it. If you can — and this demands a fair degree of concentration — put the line completely out of your mind and try to determine how you would attack the problem if the obvious solution was not there. The reason for this type of thinking is to train the mind to look at all sides of the difficulty and thus have a better chance of solving it.

Riders are like sheep. They, at times, seem to follow one another blindly even if the result is a succession of fives. If the first man to do a section under the watchful eyes of his colleagues is an ace and the others follow his example, little harm will be done. But if the rider who has not given the section enough thought, leads the rest, the results can be a disaster until a rider comes along who will rethink the problem and perhaps succeed. That rider must be you.

Right, now I've got you into the right mood to do some walking, get into the section and go through it once to get the general feel of what you are up against. Then comes trip two and here you have a series of specific jobs to do. The good rider walking a section is mentally dividing the hazard into a number of smaller problems, and, in effect, finding himself parts which we will call rest areas. These occur in practically every section and can give time for the rider to regather himself for the next tricky bit.

It's very rare in a long section for the need for continual all-out effort so use these rest zones to get things under control, to change gear if needed and to face up to the next problem.

Of course you are looking for the right line which may or may not be the obvious one, and even deciding on a not-so-copy-book attempt if such a deal fits your riding style. For it

It's impossible to spend too much time in a trial, without a speed schedule, on inspecting sections. Here a group of riders is lining up a rocky stream bed. They are choosing their path, checking for submerged rocks and trying to assess the degree of slime that could cause them trouble

A typical, innocuous-looking sandy section. But don't be fooled. Because of the loose nature of the surface it's a real mark grabber. I'm advising my pal to use the banking on the far right to help him make his turn

could be that you are a real ace on mud but no great performer on rocks and, in certain circumstances, it would be profitable to ignore a right line over a rockery and instead plough through a mud patch which holds no terrors for you but has dissuaded the rest of the entry.

Remember, too, that the right line when you first look at a section may not still be the best half-an-hour later when your turn comes. Always have a last-minute look before launching into it.

Some sections demand deliberate turns or gear changes at very definite points and here it's necessary to have some form of marker to remind yourself, once in the section, of the exact moment to make your move. Any form of landmark will do — a tree, a rock. It's even possible to use the observer if he's well encamped with a picnic stool, umbrella and thermos flask.

But, if he's the jump-about type, don't rely on his being in the same place when you get into the section. I often make a point of asking a spectator — yes, all right, a nice-looking female if possible — to stand in a specific position. I recommend this idea but don't make the big mistake I did and pick the latest girlfriend of your chief rival in the event. She knew the score and moved just a foot to one side. Not enough to make it obvious to me as I approached, but quite sufficient to turn my projected clean ride into a five.

It's also possible to play a little gamesmanship as you walk up the section. Without making it too obvious to the observer the odd kick at a loose rock to move it out of your chosen path or a stamp or two on a camber to aid wheelgrip will not go amiss. Do I hear a cry of 'cheating'? In my book it's no more cheating than the golfer who picks out an errant tuft of grass on the green. And, perhaps more to the point, everyone else is playing the same game. I don't mean take a rotovator and road roller into the section — I'm talking about a casual stroll with the odd clumsy trip that moves a rock aside.

And no observer is really going to moan about the breaking off of the odd twig which otherwise could go in an eye and cause a nasty. While on the twig subject, if you, as I did, take to a crash helmet late in your trials career, remember that you need a little more clearance under trees. I've got a lot of skid marks on the top of my helmet to remind me.

With a back-up like this it's worth having another look at the section just before your turn comes.
It could have altered dramatically in the time you have been queuing

Now we've got the whole problem of walking the section licked, it's time to make your play. It is all important to have a good approach for, without it, the best attempt in the world will fail. Make your lead-in run from just as far back as you think is necessary — always allowing there is room. Remember that you are not officially in the section until your front wheel spindle has passed the begins card and, at any time on your run-up, you can abort and go back for another attempt.

I've seen some riders make quite a mess of their run into the section but still carry on into the hazard. And when I've tackled them afterwards and asked them why they didn't take a second bite at it they replied that they didn't want to feel foolish in front of their friends. To my mind, an unnecessary five on the observer's card is a lot sillier than a second run-up and a clean.

The time will come when there just isn't enough room at a section to get the run-in you require. Here you must decide either to make your attack at a slower speed, or to burn your way into the hazard with a speedway-type start which may give you the velocity you require but with a certain loss of fine control.

At times there may be so little room before the begins card, perhaps because of a gaggle of waiting riders, that there is no way you can manoeuvre the bike to line it up for the section without actually pushing the front wheel in and then pulling it out again. A pedantic observer could levy five marks against your score for this, claiming that, as the bike had entered the section, you had made your attempt and failed.

The secret here is another little gamesmanship ploy. The system is to wait until the preceding rider has passed the observer, therefore guaranteeing the official's eyes are turned away from the start, before doing any jiggering with the machine. Don't think that I'm having a go at observers in general. I know hundreds of them and count them as friends. It's just that some follow the letter of the law rather than its spirit, and it's better to be prepared for this eventuality.

Three final points before we get onto the specific types of sections you are likely to encounter in a trial. More and more trials are becoming multi-lap affairs with the same sections used two or more times. In order to speed things up a little, I normally ask the observer on my second, and subsequent, times around whether a section has been altered in any way. If he confirms that it has not, and it presented me with no difficulties on the first attempt, I will generally tackle it without another inspection tour. However, if I lost marks the first time around, or if the observer tells me it has been toughened or eased, then it's time for a little leg-work again. Remember, too, that any drastic change in weather conditions can dramatically alter a hazard.

I'm not going to make any suggestions on the subject of baulking — whereby a rider can claim a re-run if he has been interrupted in his attempt; perhaps by a dog, running into the section or by an unwitting spectator stepping into his path. But I'll say a word of thanks to a journalist in Scotland a few years ago. High in the mountains on the notorious Laggan Locks section he was watching and saw me get into disastrous trouble. It was obvious that I was about to shudder to a standstill. Quick-wittedly he 'accidentally' kicked a camera case off the bank into my path, allowing me to claim a re-run. I did have trouble recently in Japan. There was this large snake sitting smack on my line, trying to devour a frog! I feel this should lead to a special clause in trials regulations covering such an eventuality under 'baulks'.

There's also quite a bit of gamesmanship involved between riders as they consider the problems of each section. They will be continuously discussing what gear to use. Where to change up or down and other fine points. If you want to, you can give all your secrets away, or you can try a gentle confidence trick. But remember, if you take advice from your fellow rider, that he's probably read this book as well!

The uphill climb

With a straightforward section up a hillside you are relying on the grip of the rear wheel and your angle of attack. Being in full control of the machine and correctly positioned at all times on the ascent are vital. Because of the nature of the hazard you are going to have to build up speed for your attempt. And here, not only must the section be walked, but also the ground preceding it which you will use for your run-in.

I've seen characters back off their bike almost into the next county before thundering in, working their way up the gearbox and reaching a phenomenal speed just before the begins card, only to hit a small undulation which launches them high in the air so that they come down in the middle of the hazard like the proverbial ton of bricks. Although it's clear that this system doesn't work, there's probably still a queue of people way back waiting their chance to do some bulldozing. When I line up only half the distance away to make my run-in I often get some pretty strange looks but I approach the section steadily, riding up and down any undulation so that, as I pass the begins card, my wheels are on the ground. I'm in the right gear, with the engine pulling at its best power setting to carry me to the summit.

This fine-throttle setting that we need to achieve at the point we pass the begins card is something that is really only learnt from experience.

On ascents positioning of body weight is all-important. In this shot I am much too far back and the front wheel is riding high in the air. It may look spectacular but I am short on control

And here's the opposite problem. I've got plenty of control at the front but no weight on the rear wheel which is about to start spinning - and that's the end of that attempt

The perfect solution. Body weight is just right. The trunk should be kept vertical giving sufficient grip at the back wheel without the possibility of the front end coming up

On the way up. My weight's well forward and the engine is working hard. But I'm just about ready to roll the throttle off as there is a tight left-hand turn just beyond the stakes

Will he, won't he? As it happens I did get over this steep rise and, in this case, my technique is quite good. The front wheel is on the ground ready to give maximum control for the coming descent. Practice climbs where you have flat ground at the top or you'll take off like a moon-shot until you get the hang of it

The position of the body in making an attempt is all important. A natural, relaxed stance will do as much to get you up the hill as grip from the rear tyre. If you have your weight too far back there is a danger of the front wheel rising. With the weight too far forward, grip can be lost and steering becomes difficult with the rider's arms too bent.

Standing in a relaxed manner on the rests, try to keep the body in as near a vertical line as possible. This means that as the gradient changes so must the angle between you and the bike. It is therefore clear that on a very steep ascent you will be closer to the front wheel than on a gentle incline. It is very unusual for it to be necessary to change gear on a hill. With the correct gear engaged at the start and the engine pulling strongly, there should usually be no need to go down a cog.

Unnecessary gear changing on hills invariably leads to the loss of five marks. On a really long ascent a top-class rider will get away with the odd downward change. The superstar, realising that the hill has become too steep or his speeds too slow for the gear he's using, will let the machine slow down until he can make a quick dab on the gear pedal to change down so that, in the new gear, the engine is producing its best torque. He won't be using the clutch but simply easing the throttle a little as he moves the pedal. A casual spectator would probably fail to notice that he's made the change.

The biggest mistake that beginners make is to change down too early. Doing so, they find that they are over-revving in the lower gear and that wheel spin sets in, leading to an instant stop.

There will come a time when, despite everything a rider tries he is able to go no further up a steep ascent and that he must abandon ship. On no account try to stay with the bike. To tumble down a hill with an errant bike catching you up at the bottom is no joke. By far the best method is to lay the bike, as gently as possible, onto its side, stepping off in the process. This way, neither you nor the bike are likely to come to any harm. Another golden rule — if coming gently to rest halfway up still astride — never pull in the clutch lever or you will start travelling backwards. Fast. Just let the engine stall which will hold you there.

This ultra-tight turn, after a descent and leading to a climb could not be cleaned. I pre-determined that a deliberate dab would be the minimum possibly penalty. I have my foot down early and am starting to haul the bike around

Now we're getting the bike into line. My foot is still in the same position, but, because of the severity of the turn my foot is still well forward of the machine

Half way round and still dragging the bike, forcing it to pivot around my foot

Last stage. Now the foot has ceased to be a pivot and it is going to be used to give me a little help in getting the bike moving up the incline. Note that my weight is well forward ready to cope with a rising front wheel.

Here we're in trouble. We've got nearly to the top of the hill and run out of grip. Never, never pull in the clutch or you'll set off backwards at a tremendous rate of knots to land in an undignified heap at the bottom all mixed up with the bike. If you get into trouble on a hill shut the throttle and let the engine stall. Lay the bike gently over until the handlebar and footrest digs into the ground

Stage two. Step off the bike and you and the machine have come to no harm. I usually try to lay the machine down on the lefthand side - the throttle is on the right. But if there is a drop or large boulder to the left, there's no harm in picking the alternative route

Downhill

This is one section of trials riding in which you cannot have too much practice. Although the sport is one of the safest in the world, injuries, if they do come, are nearly always from ill-managed attempts at downhill sections.

Most of the disasters come from sheer panic, and this is why it is imperative that any steep downhill section is treated coolly and with the greatest of respect. This panic can occur once or any number of times in a descent but, once you have mastered mind-over-gradient, it means you have developed exceptional self-control which will pay off in the trials game and when driving the family in the car, should an awkward situation arise.

The correct approach to any downhill hazard is of the utmost importance. Many sections, of which the most difficult part is downhill, have a climbing approach and you must plan this so you arrive at the top in full control for the descent. Leaping off the summit, both wheels in the air isn't guaranteed to enhance control on the delicate downhill path. Clearly, we will want to descend most sections as slowly as possible and this calls for delicate use of both brakes. It has been proved time and again that the maximum braking to be achieved by any vehicle is at the point just before the wheels lock. This is true on any type of surface.

Complicated anti-skidding devices have been built into experimental motor cars but these are so heavy and complicated that they are, at least in our lifetime, unlikely to be seen on any production motorcycle — let alone a spartan trials machine. Therefore, we have to provide this anti-skid mechanism with our own minds and body.

Some riders try to achieve this maximum braking by adjusting their front brake lever so that when it is pulled all the way back to the handlebar, the wheel can still not lock up. This is a highly dangerous practice as, in traffic and at a higher speed than you would use in sections, you need all the braking you can get. The idea doesn't even work very well in sections because varying surfaces will alter the locking-up tendencies of the wheel.

The answer is to develop a fine control so that you can hold the brakes just off the locking-up stage. Your reflexes will then let you quickly ease pressure should the wheel start to lock. This all sounds very difficult but with practice — which can be on a simple, non-frightening slope — you'll be surprised how quickly the art can be developed.

On very steep descents I advocate that the clutch should be held in and the throttle kept sufficiently open to keep the engine turning over. This prevents any chance of the engine being stalled if the back wheel is accidentally locked up.

Now this sort of rodeo act is the result of not following my own advice. OK, I was able to leap aboard the bike as it came down on two wheels and ride it to the bottom. Unless you've got quite a few years of trials behind you, you won't be equipped for this sort of performance just yet

Front-brake technique. You can use one, two, three or four fingers on the brake lever depending upon the efficiency of the stopper and the severity of the descent

The clutch lever should be held with three fingers as shown leaving the thumb, palm and index-finger to firmly grip the bar

With the thumb and index-finger held as shown you need have no worries about keeping control

Now put the hand-hold together and, with foot brake control, practise a lot

I know that many accomplished riders will disagree with the clutch-in advice, arguing that it is difficult to take up the drive when nearing the bottom of the hill and claiming that the transition between having the clutch in and letting it out can lead to a loss of control.

There can be some truth in this but my system overcomes the problems. I start down the hill with the clutch lever held against the bar but, as I approach the bottom of the incline, facing, perhaps, a tight turn and a climb, I gradually feed in the clutch and ease open the throttle, letting the engine work against the brakes. This way the bike stays taut, I'm in control and, at the point where I need to accelerate, the machine is ready to do so. Again this idea of working the engine against the brakes can be practised on the shallowest of slopes or, for that matter, on flat ground. And of course my system allows the bike to be in the correct gear for the following part of the hazard — something not always possible when a gear has to be chosen for a decline.

In all this talk on slowing the machine on hills I have purposely spoken of brakes in the plural for the front stopper, avoided like the plague by some novices, is all important. With the front wheel considerably lower than the rear, it's the forward brake that's going to do most of the work.

The reason why a beginner avoids the front brake is that he has great difficulty in recovering if the wheel locks up. The lightest over application of the front stopper and the novice is over on his ear. This may have something to do with his failure to release the brake in time but is more likely to be a result of incorrect stance. If the machine is correctly lined up, with the wheels absolutely vertical, a front-wheel lock-up can be coped with easily.

Stance will also play a big part in downhill control. As we have said, ideally we try to keep the front wheel vertical in relation to the terrain but we must also maintain equal pressure on each side of the handlebar or, again, a slight locking up of the front wheel will send the rider off at the side he was exerting most pressure. The best way to achieve this is with the elbows locked straight.

Never being one for hurting myself needlessly, I treat all downhill sections with caution and that means never giving up when it looks like danger is looming. I'm not talking about saving marks now but saving a tangled mass of bike and rider at the bottom of the hill.

When things get out of control on a steep downhill section and it looks as if a crash is inevitable, don't panic. You can't abandon ship halfway down so you've got to stay with the bike as long as possible. More times than I care to remember, I've been in a situation where all looks lost, only to pull something out of the bag at the last minute. Look at it this way; you are getting out of control and have played all the techniques mentioned so far. They are not helping at all. The bike's going faster and faster and you are getting frightened out of your skin. Now, on these rare occasions, it's time to try the Don Smith master plan. Why not, you have got nothing to lose?

Its worked for me many times and I'll probably have to use it again. The plot is to tread the bike into a higher gear and get the throttle open. I know it's against all natural instincts, but if you ever have to try it, you'll be surprised to find that it can help get back to the ideal situation of you controlling the bike instead of it controlling you.

And one gear may not be enough. For, if you started out in first and you are up to 25 or 30 miles per hour when you decide to try the stunt, second gear would obviously not do the trick and you would have to hook the pedal up to third or even fourth as you feed home the clutch.

More often than not you will get away with it. Sure, you have probably missed the markers but you're still on the bike and you and the machine are unscathed. On the odd occasion that even this ploy fails to deliver the goods, there's only one thing left to do — pray.

One other form of descent must come within the scope of this section. That is the short, sharp drop over a bank, a hazard much enjoyed by those who mark out courses and sections. These over-the-ledge hazards fall into two groups. Both must be tackled with a very deliberate stance. The front wheel must be kept absolutely straight or it will tuck under and you'll sail through the air over the handlebars. Arms should be locked straight, again with equal pressure

This is the problem. A steepish drop with a sharp turn at the bottom and a re-climb. I'm near stationary at the top aiming at the slowest possible descent so that I can pick my position for the left hairpin

On the way down. The forks are fully depressed under the effect of braking and I'm looking well ahead to line up the problem to come. Note that the bike is vertical and that my arms are braced

Even gentle banks should be treated with respect and given the straight-arm, weight-well-back technique

Off the banking in the last section. My arms are rigid and my seat well back over the rear wheel. Note that the front forks are fully depressed

on each arm. To prevent any tendency for the bike to cartwheel over the front wheel, your body weight should be kept well back with the seat of your pants near the saddle or rear fender.

Some drops are too sharp, or even undercut, to allow a bike to roll over them and the front wheel must then be jumped out to land further forward than it would do if the machine were merely rolled over the top. To do this the bike must be gently accelerated off the ledge. Only two types of going make nonsenses of the general rules for descending hills.

When dropping down the side of a sand-covered bank it is vital that the machine is kept under power. Otherwise, sand will build up forward of the front wheel until, eventually, you have an unclimbable barrier which will send you down the rest of the section ahead of the bike. Because of the power absorbing nature of sand, a fairly low gear will be necessary for such manoeuvres. In soft sand there is no real chance of your speed building up and you will find that you have to use as much throttle to go downhill as up a similar gradient with a harder surface.

The bank is too undercut to allow me to roll off it so I have pushed the front wheel out with gentle use of the throttle. Note that my arms are rigid to stop the front wheel tucking under and my weight is to the back so that there's no chance of the rear of the machine coming up

Faced with a steep drop and an ultra-tight turn inside the markers, this competitor made one big mistake. He forgot to dry out his brakes from the previous water splash and sailed merrily on at the bottom

The other type of going which requires a power descent is loose rocks. Try to ride these too slowly or with the brakes on and you will find that they are like marbles underneath the front wheel, ready to flick it to one side so quickly that you have no chance of recovering. When descending on such going use a fairly high gear so that there is less chance of the back wheel locking up. Take the bike down steadily on a small throttle opening. Also, if you need to increase the momentum of the bike you will do so more markedly in a higher ratio.

A rocky descent calls for throttle work. Note that I am not touching the clutch lever as I am driving the bike down under power

Mud

Mud comes in a larger variety of mixes than a wallowing hippopotamus ever dreamed of, so we will deal with them one by one. The brand of mud least feared by the trials rider is the virgin variety which the lucky men at the head of the entry alone see. This is normally no problem. With a slightly higher gear than you would use for the same section in the dry, you will find that the surface gives fairly good grip. It is important to have some degree of speed but it is amazing at the traction that can be found in a high cog (second or third) even when the bike is almost at a standstill, and using only a wisp of throttle.

The same section for the man at the end of the entry can provide a very different set of problems. He will either find a great sea of churned black glue or a long series of footrest-deep ruts. The sea of mud can only be approached at the highest possible speed in the highest possible gear. Just how fast and how high a gear depends on (a) how much of a run you can get and (b) your guts and riding ability.

With the footrest-deep ruts, sufficient of a run is necessary to aviate the front wheel so that the rests do not clog into the mud. This is not as difficult as it sounds and if you practice the ploy you will find that the secret will soon come.

Perhaps surprisingly, a long shallow rut is much more of a problem, for the front wheel is continually trying to climb up one side or the other. A rider's natural answer to this is to strengthen his grip on the bar and to turn into the direction the wheel wants to take him. That's his first mistake. The answer is to relax and loosen the grip on the bars sufficiently to let the wheel go where it pleases. For it must follow the rut. Now all you've got to do is keep the bike upright, which is a combination of balance and throttle control — the very things you started to practice in your garage the day your first bike was delivered.

The term bottomless mud is probably inaccurate, but ask any novice, with his bike stuck solid up to the carburettor in the sticky black goo, just how deep it is, and that's the answer he will give you.

There's only one way to ride such a section and that's to take the bike back just as far as you can, work up the highest possible speed and launch yourself into it. If there is a small undulation which can get you off the ground before you hit the mud, all well and good. But remember, do not use the motocross trick of shutting the throttle as the back wheel leaves the ground. When you plough into that mud you want everything going for you. And that includes an engine with the twistgrip open wide. Don't worry about over-revving the engine, a modern bike can take that sort of punishment in its stride.

Glorious mud. I've got a front wheel riding high and am using every ounce of power, the 250 cc Greeves can deliver

A fine example of a muddy slot. I'm staying loose and letting the bike find its own way through. The throttle is well open and mud is spraying out from the back wheel. I remember the event well - an international, called the St. Cucufa - just five miles outside Paris. At this period of my career I won ten consecutive major European International Trials - it made a nice poster for Greeves!

Once into the mire, keep the throttle full open. You are hanging off the back of the bike to give the rear wheel maximum bite, your engine is screaming, you're throwing a hundred-foot stream of mud into the sky behind you and it's the greatest fun in the world.

It's amazing how full throttle can sometimes get you out of problems. Often, on many types of going, when all looks lost, a quick twist of the throttle to the flat-out position can sometimes save the day. But beware for, as the bike crawls on at one mile an hour with the back wheel doing 30, a sudden helping of grip can send the machine skyward like a moon probe.

A layer of wet mud on top of a firmer surface gives even the superstars maximum aggravation. All you can do is copy them in making sure that they are accurately lined up for the hazard and with sufficient speed to drastically reduce the amount of time they spend in the section. It's on this type of going that the full-throttle treatment can often save a five, but remember there's a hard surface underneath which can provide that sudden, embarrassing bite.

Even worse than surface mud is muddy slime on rocks. The only secret here is moderate speed and to ride square over everything.

For mud use the lowest possible tyre pressures. The actual pressure will depend on your weight, but if you use five pounds per square inch for rocks you would want to drop to three for mud.

I'm a great believer in low tyre pressures. It was often said, when we used the old, heavier 4-ply covers, that when I unscrewed the inner tube valve the air rushed *in*.

It shouldn't be necessary to state the obvious but, after watching some riders in muddy trials, I'll point out the need for ensuring that your wheels are free to turn before attempting a section. Some mud is of a very clinging type and will jam up around the fork legs and chain guard to such an extent that, unless cleared away with a stick, will absorb a good 50 per cent of the engine power you are trying to deliver to the ground.

Chalk

Dry chalk provides few problems for an experienced rider. It gives lots of grip, but watch out when you are walking the section for any loose patches which can cause the front wheel to twitch. Such a twitch is no great problem if you are riding loose and relaxed.

Wet chalk is a different kettle of fish and can be the most difficult of all surfaces on which to ride. The only man with any decent chance is the one at the front of the entry who may find a little grip. But, after a few riders have passed, the surface, which seems to act like blotting paper to water, develops about as much grip as a jelly on a skating rink. With a little luck some form of rut may develop which will help or a small path be formed on a camber but, if not, you will have to throw all the textbook techniques out of the window, take the bike back into the next county and go into the section with, hopefully, enough speed to get you beyond the ends card before you land on your ear.

Rocks

Rocks, like mud, come in many shapes and designs, each demanding a different approach.

Large rocks, firmly embedded in the ground, are little problem to the late runners but, if slime covered, can be very slippery for the early numbers. Either way, a rock should be approached as squarely as possible and the bike lifted over it in the same way as over that log in your driveway. It's on this sort of section that you will begin to find out whether your front forks are correctly set up. It is all important that you have the correct grade and amount of oil for your weight and the climate. With too thin an oil in the damping mechanism, the wheel will dance about all over the place and, if the oil is too heavy, it will be like riding a machine with two rigid bean poles out in front. Either way, the bike will be unsteerable. But with the forks set up correctly you find yourself achieving what you earlier thought impossible.

The same is true for the rear suspension, but often grades and amounts of oil are determined by the manufacturer who provides a sealed, unadjustable unit.

I believe in fairly soft damping at the rear of a machine as this helps the tyre stay in contact with the ground and allows the suspension to return to its unloaded position, ready for the next bump, more easily.

Wherever possible, ride straight over rocks rather than attempting to wriggle round them. In this section the ends cards were immediately to the left and any attempt to use, what looks to be an easier line, at the left of the large boulder would have prevented a tight-enough turn

On loose rocks, grip is at a minimum — as it is on loose slate. A high gear, reasonable turn of speed and the machine correctly set up in the vertical position, should be coupled with a deliberate and aggressive riding style. You have to demonstrate that you are mastering the machine and preventing its natural skittishness and desire to go its own way.

Large rock steps take us back to our driveway log again, but here we must be extra careful. For, although the undersides of trial machines are rigidly built with strong sump shields, they do not take over-kindly to continual smashing on granite. Therefore, after you have graduated from the log, practice on small, and then larger fallen trees before graduating to the hard stuff.

All may look lost but what, in fact, has happened is that I have run off my path and am giving away a dab deliberately to enable me to pivot the bike back, around its rear wheel and my foot, into the stream-bed section

You don't normally find this amount of grip on loose boulders and, I'll admit, this took me by surprise. Loose boulders should be tackled with speed and aggression. But be ready for the odd surprise like this

More Hawks Nest terror. It is important to remember that you must judge a section as a whole and sometimes take a more difficult path to enable you to line up for the problem to come

On rocks it is necessary to keep the bike vertical, riding over problems rather than trying to go around them

A glorious section. The natural rock hazard of Hawks Nest is the Peak District. No need for tape here - just the odd marker

Never be over-worried about having the odd dab. In a tough enough trial there will always be opportunities of recovering your position later

Cambers

When crossing a camber the thing to do is — nothing abruptly, and everything gently. Have faith in the ability of your machine and its tyres to hang on to near-impossible angles and, when walking the section, watch out for any little embedded stone or tree root which could provide that little extra aid in straightening the machine if it seems about ready to slip downwards.

If the bike begins to take it into its own mind to head down the camber when you want to go across, and there is sufficient room between the lines of markers, allow it to do so for a little before taking another bite at getting the machine lined up.

When walking the section always be on the look-out for a way of reducing the negative camber. I've seen sections which have been laid out with an obvious negative camber in view but, by lining up the machine differently can be turned into an easy wall-of-death ride.

On cambers such as this it is imperative to keep the bike vertical. I'm trying not to blink an eyelid for any movement can send the bike down the slope

The same problem in reverse. Remember to look for any protrusion which can help keep the bike on your chosen path

Nadgery

Non-English readers seeing the word nadgery may well be excused if they have little idea of what it means. I have no idea of its derivation but any English trials rider will tell you that nadgery is tight-turning, threading through small gaps — in fact the type of section predominant in the wooded South and East of Britain.

The secret of success on this type of going comes from a relaxed stance, delicate throttle control and microscopically-accurate positioning. Some clerks of the course seem to design these sections taking into account the minimum turning circle of the machine. Therefore if you are one inch out in making your turn, instead of getting round, you finish up in a tree.

Walking the section can sometimes be harrowing, for many of them look just too tight to be possible. But the seasoned rider will stay cool and be ready to take advantage of any help that a protruding tree root or other natural mound will give him.

I am leaning on that branch! (250 Greeves, Kickham Trophy, March 1966)

It is in nadgery sections that quite a few arguments develop over whether a rider has actually stopped and whether he has used a tree to render a little 'outside assistance'. As these sections are normally the slowest to be found in the trials game, the decisions of an observer over whether a rider has actually stopped are, quite understandably, sometimes disputed. Even a novice rider can stand still on the footrests for quite a period. And, whilst most regulations allow for a 'momentary halt', no one is going to expect an official to allow you to stop long enough to light another cigarette.

With the predominance of trees in nadgery sections there is often a great temptation for a rider to use his shoulder against one to help keep the bike upright. Technically this constitutes a dab. But if you're quick enough, who knows, you may get away with it.

Here, I am supporting the tree trunk! (250 Kawasaki, Sidcup Trial, January 1974)

Stream beds

I always treat any section which is under-water with the greatest respect, especially if I have an early number and know that any rocks at the bottom may still be covered in slippery slime.

Don't be afraid to get your feet wet — and that means walking through the water, however deep, to find exactly the best path for your machine. Again make a point of finding landmarks which will indicate any particularly deep holes or hidden rocks. And remember, even a deep pool can have its own rock at the bottom waiting to slip your front wheel to one side.

A certain amount of speed in such going is necessary if the bike is to be kept in a reasonably straight line. But, for the inexperienced, too much velocity will obviously end in a too-early Sunday night bath.

Water splashes

For some strange reason, clerks of the course seem to delight in directing the competitors through deep water splashes and even marking out sections where the depth of the water is the only real hazard. I've never seen the point in deep water sections, especially if there is plenty of grip and a flat surface underneath.

There is always a grave danger of doing the engine considerable harm if water is sucked up the exhaust pipe, and such sections seem to prove little, other than which machine has the highest air intake to the carburettor.

If you are faced with water splashes of any type with a good surface underneath, the secret is to take them as slowly as possible. There is no point in setting up a bow wave like the USS America — you'll only send water everywhere risking a drowned engine and a wet pair of pants for the rest of the event.

After going through such a ford remember to dry out your brakes by gentle application of both levers or you could enter the next section with a bike that won't slow down at all.

How not to ride water

How to ride water

Sand

This type of section is where you get your own back on the bike, take out the frustrations on your wife who was late getting ready that morning and your annoyance with the neighbour who still has your lawnmower he borrowed a month ago. Because, in sand you are going to be forceful, deliberate and downright aggressive.

Sand has one nasty habit. It tends to build up in front of you like a wall. And any shilly-shallying, pussy-footing delicateness is going to bring you to a sudden stop against that wall of sand, or send you over the bars.

Any turn that you have to make must be planned beforehand and viciously executed under power. Trying to ease the bike around gently will bring about that instant build-up against the front wheel which will, surprisingly, tend to pitch you suddenly into the corner and not, as one would think, over the handlebars.

To prevent this build-up against the banked-over front wheel, try to keep the bike as vertical as possible using body lean on the corners to help get you round. Here again, any natural banking or grass tufts which tend to firm-up the surface should be used for making the turns rather than trying to force the bike around on the loose stuff.

Long blasts through deep sand call for the same recipe as for deep mud. Except that, because of the power sapping characteristics of sand, you need a lower gear and, if possible, more revs. Hitting loose sand unexpectedly is like having both brakes lock on at once. Therefore you must go into the section as quickly as possible, blasting your way through and attempting to keep the front wheel riding as lightly as possible to prevent the dreaded build-up.

The same loose sand section, after one hundred competitors have blasted through, will have changed dramatically. All that low gear work will have churned up a long, deep rut. And that's good. Now the back wheel will probably bite through to something resembling grip. And you don't have the worry of having to aviate the front wheel to keep the foot-rests clear — the loose sand on the surface will simply be brushed away by the rests and, therefore, not impede your progress.

Don't lose the front wheel like this

Also, should you wish to change from one rut to another, it is a lot easier to do so in sand than in mud. But, remember, again it is necessary to be aggressive and deliberate or the sand build-up will win the battle for control.

Of all sections you are likely to meet whilst competing in trials, those which use sand are most likely to favour the late numbers. I have ridden in events run over two laps of the same course where, on the first circuit, the sections were next to impossible and on the second time around no more difficult than the Massachusetts turnpike. Therefore, it's obvious that a late number is a tremendous advantage. The man running at the rear of the entry does his sections in what are, virtually, second-lap conditions. Whereas, the rider at the front of the field has to blaze a trail for the other competitors.

Other problems

Other problems which you are likely to meet, including wet grass, and leaf mould are, in effect, really combinations of those problems we have dealt with above. If you learn to master the techniques needed for the basic types of sections, nothing else will hold any fears for you.

One of the greatest trials riders, Yorkshire's Malcolm Rathmell, is an expert at the big dab. His policy, and it's one worth following, is *if you're going to put a foot down and lose a mark, get the most benefit from it.*

He specialises in being able to ascertain just where he will need a dab — and in making it in such a determined fashion that he will get as much help from it as some other riders will from five minutes wild flaying with both feet.

When you dab, dab well! (250 Montesa, Mitchell Trial, September 1968). I came second

The deliberate dab is of particular use when making an ultra-tight turn. The body should be moved up the bike and the leg extended to its very maximum before putting it to ground. The bike can then be ridden around the foot which only comes off the ground as the back wheel passes.

The same can hold true of footing. Once you have lost three marks in a section there is very little point in attempting to clean the rest of it if there is any danger of a five. Far better to keep making like a windmill with the size 10s until you are past the ends markers.

Feet down, bottom well back

The very deliberate dab can also have an extraordinary side effect. Picture the scene. A superstar approaches a particularly difficult section of the course, where the observer has seen a couple of dozen lesser lights come to an undignified halt. The superstar comes through. As he reaches the critical point, his machine too stops but, in a flash, his whole body lunges forward, a foot thrusts out, the engine revs soar, and he's through, still moving. So bemused by the whole circus trick, the observer doesn't register in his mind that the bike actually stopped at all and his pencil makes one penalty mark on his card instead of the five that maybe it was.

This time on a 250 Montesa - lots of power - Victory Trial, February 1970

Because observers are human they do make errors and organisers, appreciating this, make provision in the regulations of an event for the rider to be able to protest against any decision.

To guard against frivolous moaning, the organisers usually insist each protest is accompanied by a cash deposit which is refundable only if the claim is upheld — or denied, but found to be reasonable.

In England each event has a number of stewards, some appointed by the club and others by the Auto-Cycle Union which governs all motorcycle sport in the country. Protests, which must be made within a stipulated time following the publication of the results, are heard by this group who make a decision on evidence given by the rider, any witnesses he may call and the observer in question.

No one likes protesting. For years I fought against many inclinations to put in my money after a blatant mistake had robbed me of an award. Some consider any form of protest as an unsportsmanlike action but, particularly in the case of a works rider, they are sometimes inevitable. The factory-sponsored competitor has to produce results to earn his money and the continued support he enjoys. It is, therefore, quite reasonable that he should make an attempt to have an error rectified.

Of course, the ideal way to allow for observer error is to win the trial by such a vast margin that any mistake **can be accepted.**

I'm not suggesting that everyone becomes a barrack-room lawyer but it is to any rider's advantage that he has studied the regulations before the start of the event. Faced with a dangerous-looking hazard the novice rider should know, in advance, whether opting out of an attempt will cost him five marks, ten marks or exclusion. It is quite possible that no one else will be able to give him the information.

It's quite reasonable that our novice rider will think it better to lose five marks than risk his bike, and a chance of finishing, on a section about which he's not confident. However, if he has read the regulations and knows that *failure to attempt the section shall be exclusion*, it's quite obvious that he has to make some kind of effort, even if it is only the token gesture of pushing his front wheel through the begins cards and taking a five.

Given a little time I can search through my dusty attic and find the diary in which I entered details of my first year's riding career.

In it I detailed sending off for regulations, making my entry, the result obtained, and my brief impression of the event. I advise you to do the same. Having a permanent record of one's performance, apart from making interesting fireside reading, gives you an indication of how you are progressing.

Another advantage of keeping a diary is that you lessen the chance of entering two events on the same day. Double entries are not only foolish, in that they cost you two fees, but you then have the embarrassing job of explaining to the organisers just why you did not turn up, for one of them. It is also a disciplinary offence under A-CU rules.

In recent years the special test has all but disappeared from the trials scene — and not a bad thing too. Nowadays ties are usually decided by giving the award either to the man who completed the largest number of sections without loss of marks or the rider who got furthest round the course before being penalised.

However, there are still events where the organisers throw in a test where sheer speed over a short course is used as a decider. As you may have gathered, I don't like such tests but obviously you'll have to go along with the organisers and do your best to put up a good time.

Although I've taken great pains to explain that a modern-day trials bike is a well-engineered machine, adjustments do have to be made and some tools should be taken on even the shortest trial. But don't go overboard on the whole idea. I've seen some competitors laden down with half the equipment of an Indianapolis pit area and enough spares to stock an average dealer's showroom. Some of the parts they carry would take a couple of men a full day to fit and they are simply weighing themselves down needlessly.

Conversely you always meet the man who considers that everyone else in the trial should keep his bike running. He starts each event without a tool or spare, and borrows the equipment as he needs it along the route. And, judging from the small amount he usually gives back, he has probably got an enormous box at home labelled 'OPT' — other people's tools!

Ideally, your selection of tools should depend upon the length of the event you are about to encounter. Long-distance events over very rough terrain obviously demand a much larger selection than a small one-lap dash around the local farmer's number three meadow. Some tools are vital whatever the event. In the 'must' collection should be a spare plug, a spanner to put it in with, chain links, a small adjustable spanner, a tyre pressure gauge and, perhaps, a pair of tyre levers and the necessary inner tube.

Leave the big end bearing and the gearbox mainshaft at home — if you need them you're out of the race anyway.

I'd like to see every rider carry his own small toolkit and almost feel like advocating that you never loan tools during an event. If you give another rider your spare plug he's unlikely ever to provide his own if he knows he can always scrounge one. And what happens if later in the same event you need a plug yourself? This trials game of ours is essentially friendly and I guess I, and you, will go on lending tools to the thoughtless.

For something as long and difficult as the Scottish Six Days Trial, your toolkit will obviously go up, with a bang. The Scottish rider, as well as the items mentioned above, will probably have spare spokes, a duplicate rear chain, and a mass of other similar items which, his experience tells him, he may require.

I made it this time. Leaves are difficult (250 Montesa, Cotswold Cup, December 1968)

10
After the trial

Picture the scene. You've just come back from a rather tough day out in a very muddy trial. You are covered in dirt from head to foot and the bike's just a heaving mass of filth. Got the picture? Good, we'll carry on.

Back at home you strip off, shower, wheel the bike into the middle of the lawn, turn on the hose and settle down in a hammock with the latest Arthur Haley and a long cool gin fizz while the lawn sprinkler plays idly over the machine. You nod off and when you awake the dinner is ready, there's a fresh drink at your hand and the bike looks showroom new.

Like the idea? Good. Now forget it.

A lawn sprinkler or even a casually held hosepipe jet isn't going to bring back that factory shine. When you get back from an event it's time to pay out a little for all that pleasure with a spot of work. Don't get frightened, with the right approach and equipment the task can be almost fun.

Methods of cleaning can vary from a high-pressure jet to a bucket in the street — I've tried them all. The important thing is to get the bike really clean.

I take cleaning the bike almost as seriously as I do riding it and over the years have collected an assortment of handy-shaped brushes that would make the employees of any Hilton washing-up room green with envy. For, although cleaning the bike is not an onerous chore for me, I do like to make things as easy as possible.

I've got a special brush for the spokes, another for the hubs and a supersoft item for the tank and other paintwork. I'm not going to tell you how and what brushes to use - to tell the truth I've forgotten the origins of some of them, but once you've spent half an hour cleaning a bike you'll know exactly what you look for in the local hardware shop.

Right, you're set, but there's another important factor. It's all too easy to get home after a fun day, push the bike to the rear of the garage and collapse into that hammock. After all, you tell yourself, you probably won't want to use it again for another week and that gives you plenty of time.

Well, if you have money to burn and don't mind doubling the cleaning work involved you are on a winner. But my bikes are reckoned to last quite a while and there are other things I'd rather do than clean off mud, therefore I make it a point to attack the bike the minute I get home.

In this way I score twice. Firstly, the mud is probably still wet and not baked onto the bike. Secondly, harmful road salts and even fertilizer which can attack aluminium will not have a chance to do their evil work.

Although not exorbitantly expensive you can't buy a trials bike with a handful of trading stamps. And it therefore makes sense to look after your investment. When I was a dealer, specialising in trials machines, I was sometimes appalled at the state of some of the bikes offered to me in part exchange. Although less than 12 months old they were battered and beaten and looked more like World War I despatch rider mounts which had crossed a minefield than 'just-used'

This could be the state of your bike after a trial

The best cleaning equipment

With very little dismantling you can remove the air cleaner and stuff a rag into the carburetter opening to prevent too much water getting in

My selection of brushes. Each has a specific job

A stiff brush is useful for tough jobs like the rear suspension springs

An angled brush comes in handy for jobs like this

Paintwork calls for a soft brush and gentle action

Clean finning always makes a bike look like new

Make cleaning the riding gear a regular part of the post-trial performance

samples. And the amount of money I was able to allow for trade-in against a new model, there-fore, dropped appreciably.

Cleaning a bike is a lot less of a chore than a few years ago for nowadays engine cases are more streamlined and offer fewer pockets in which mud can be trapped. There's really no point in a designer building a super-light machine if it's going to accumulate 30 lbs of mud the first time it hits the dirt. Nor with today's brake linings and more efficient waterproofing of hubs is it necessary to dismantle the hubs, after washing down, to dry them out.

When hosing down the bike be sure to direct the jet all over the machine and that means laying the bike on one side and then the other to ensure that the mud comes off from every-where. With all the bulk dirt removed, the brushes come into play. What you are trying to do in effect is to rub the brush over every part of the machine; then with a final rinse, you'll get that sparkling clean look that the bike enjoyed when you loaded it up that morning.

With the bike clean — and if the foregoing sounds like a long job, don't be put off, it's surprising how quickly it can be done — it's time to do a little maintenance. Not a lot, but if you are going in for serious competitions you need every little edge that a sweetly-performing machine can give you.

This gives you some idea of just how clean your machine should be before you take it to the next event. I'm pointing out the wire spiral which prevents the clutch from being over-heated by the cylinder

I'm proud of this simple bike stand which enables the machine to be twisted around through 360° and also keeps both wheels off the ground. It is better, even, than an hydraulic platform. The bike is light enough to lift the few inches off the ground if necessary to get the stand under the crank case. A hydraulic platform or any fixed stand takes up a lot of room and, remembering that you are often wanting the wheels out of a trials bike, you probably finish up with a stand such as mine on top of another stand. Keep things simple

Check the brakes and take a look at the tyres — especially the rear to see whether the leading edges of the blocks have worn round and lost their bite. It's against the rules to take a knife to the tyre to slice a section of rubber away so, if the cover is past its prime, you can either fit a new one or turn the tyre round so that the still-complete trailing edge can do a turn of duty as the leading edge. This way you can halve your tyre bills and that can't be all bad.

Don't be scared about changing a tyre. I'll admit that 10 years ago, when four-ply canvas-and-rubber tyres were very stiff, it was not the easiest job in the world but today with two or three-ply nylon-and-rubber covers the job is child's play.

Although these new, supple tyres can be put on by hand, I go against all the rules and use a pair of levers all the way. They are good quality, narrow and highly-polished levers and make the job just that little bit easier. Often when a character watches me do a tyre change I'll get a few well-meaning words of advice centred around levers not being needed and about how I am certain to rip the tube. All I can say is that I've been swapping tyres for an awful lot of years and haven't ripped one yet.

Methinks, having gone out on a limb like that, I'll have to be very, very careful next time I get the levers in my hand.

Still with the wheels, after you have had a new bike for a few weeks it is possible that the spokes will loosen up a little. Have them re-tightened and the wheels trued and the resulting job should last the life of the machine. It's also worth keeping an eye on the inner tube valve which protrudes from the wheel rim. With the very low tyre pressures used for trials work it's quite likely that the tyre will creep around the rim a little taking the inner tube with it and straining the valve which will cant sideways.

Contrary to what you might suppose, the tyre tends to creep more under braking than when accelerating.

The air filter should be removed and the element serviced. There's not a lot that can be done with paper elements, other than blowing them out from the inside — blowing from the outside will only drive the dust further in. However, most filter elements are now made of plastic foam and can be washed in petrol and then re-oiled as per the instruction book.

It's possible, if the trial was very wet or if you were a little too enthusiastic with the hose, that water has got into the carburettor, so it's always worth, as part of the post-event tune-up session, draining the carb and cleaning out the float bowl.

The chain should be adjusted and lubricated. You can indulge in the messy business with a can of grease melting on a stove and smelling something like the discharge from the local gas works or simply run an oil can over the chain, letting the lubricant seep between the side-plates and the rollers.

Modern chain lubricants work so well that it is no longer necessary to boil the chain in special grease

Some machines feature capacity-discharge ignition systems and do away with the job of adjusting the points in the flywheel magneto. If your bike has a contact breaker system with points, the gap and condition of the faces must be inspected regularly.

When checking the bike over for the next event, pay particular attention to the condition of the control cables, ensuring that they are in good order. When fitting new cables I suggest that you use, subject to availability, those now manufactured with a nylon sleeve between the inner wire and the outer casing. This is particularly important for the throttle where you want the minimum of friction and therefore the maximum feel coming through the twist grip.

Cables should be fitted so there is no danger of them being kinked or trapped in the front fork lock-stop. Immediately after fitting a new throttle cable, start the engine and hold at a steady tick-over. Turn the bars slowly from one side to the other through their full travel, and check that the engine does not speed up or slow down during the manoeuvre. It's most embarrassing to be in a tricky section and making an ultra-slow turn to have the engine rev up underneath you.

I always make a point of going over the bike with a spray lubricant as a final job. And when I say going over it, I do mean all over. For, as well as lubricating the essential pivots and cables the spray also provides a protective film which, apart from anything else, makes it easier to get the mud off next time. All right, I'll be honest, that sheen also makes it look as if I'd spent a lot longer polishing the bike than I really had. But there is one thing certain — my bike is always immaculate under that spray sheen.

That just about covers the routine maintenance but, as you become more proficient, you will find that you also become more demanding and automatically take an interest in the mechanical side of the bike. For example, the book of words that comes with the model will state just how much oil and of what type, the front forks require. That's fine for a start but, as you become more experienced you will want to experiment and, in time, it will become important to get the oil just right for you and the climate in which you ride.

Very hot weather can demand a heavier grade of oil and thinner lubricant is often necessary in colder climates. Even your weight is important, with heavier riders needing more oil in the forks than do smaller riders.

You will also discover the vast difference that one size of carburettor jet can make. I always make a point of going over the carburation of my bikes in great detail — it's amazing the difference it can make. My system is to weaken down the carburation until the bike runs perfectly cleanly at the maximum revs. Then I increase the main jetting by one stage which will prevent the engine from just revving out at full throttle but still giving maximum response to the twist grip. The pilot and other settings are equally important.

The tightness of security bolts should be checked at regular intervals. Their purpose is to prevent the tyre creeping around the rim and achieve this by clamping the inner edge of the side walls into the well of the rim. Other devices for preventing creep include serrated well walls in the rim and screws driven through the edge of the rim into the wall of the tyre.

If the above is beginning to sound just a little over technical to the raw novice, don't panic. Get to grips with the sport and within weeks you'll be talking — and understanding — like an expert.

11 Running a trial

Doubtless when you are becoming reasonably proficient in the trials game you will either join a club or, if there is not one in your area, even form one.

And it won't be long before your club decides to put on its own event for the benefit of its own members as well as those of other clubs in the area. The very success of your club could depend on the nature of that first event. If it gives good sport to all, the guys and girls will want to come back for more but, if the event is a flop, the whole gang will be off to another contest next time.

Organisation

Regulations and entry forms should be sent out as early as possible to give riders a fair chance to plan their calendars in advance. As soon as an entry is accepted, or rejected, the would-be competitor should be informed at once. There's nothing quite so aggravating as sending off an entry and then, only a couple of days before the event, get it returned with a note that the trial is over-subscribed. By then it's too late to put your name down for another trial. All a rider does in that situation is to vow not to get mixed up with that particular club again if it can possibly be avoided.

One quick hint. Make it very clear that no entries will be entertained unless they are accompanied by three stamped, addressed envelopes. A trial can easily have 200 riders — some have more — and each competitor will need to be contacted three times: to acknowledge his entry; to forward a programme with start times and other details; to send the final results. Without the entrant furnishing the finished envelopes, that's 600 names and addresses that someone will have to write. I know trials organisers and their helpers are the keenest people alive but there are limits.

Perhaps the most important official is the Clerk of the Course whose responsibility is to lay out the sections. It's not an easy number for he has to cope with a wide variety of talents from raw beginners, seasoned riders and the real experts.

Ideally the answer is to run three trials at once with three grades of section. I will never forget the days when I left local events for the big time trials and stood, mouth open and white-faced at the sheer magnitude of the section I was supposed to attempt.

Although I've said that one man, the Clerk of the Course, is responsible for layout of the sections he should have at least two helpers. If our clerk is a top expert, with him should go a raw novice and a man whose ability lies somewhere between the two.

This way there will be something for everyone in the event. All too often trials are run in which every section is a real frightener to the novice, or, conversely, a main road cakewalk to the expert. With sections graded small, medium and large in order of severity everyone, knowing which group they are slotted into, will have a good day testing their ability without being either frightened or bored.

This deal works out particularly well for the non-experts who get a chance to see what is expected of the top riders and just how tough sections should be tackled. And there's plenty of

Trials organisers in Britain go to great lengths to maintain cordial relationships with local land-owners. During the foot-and-mouth cattle epidemic of 1967, many clubs hosed down all tyres with disinfectant before machines were allowed to start. The bike I'm riding is a 250 cc Bultaco, and the picture was taken during one of my spells 'between factories'

incentive around for a rider to improve and move up a grade.

Trials must have easy sections to attract the novice and hazards tough enough to test the top riders. In trials it's no good being a big fish in a small pool and a club should encourage its top men to swim out into the big wide world and take on the best from the next county or state.

A common mistake for a club running its first trial is to under-estimate the manpower necessary for a smoothly organised event. Boss-man of the whole enterprise is the Secretary of the Meeting whose job it is to deal with all the necessary paper-work — posting entry forms, regulations, liaison with land-owners and police, and generally making sure that everything runs smoothly.

The man responsible for marking out the route is the Clerk of the Course. One enthusiast with a reasonable mechanical knowledge should be given the title of Machine Examiner and detailed the job of looking over all machines at the start to ensure that they are legal, if public roads are to be used, and do not present a safety hazard to the spectator. This man also has the unenviable task of ensuring that all machines are reasonably silenced and of excluding any anti-social screamers. You will also need a diligent and enthusiastic results team built up of men who will, if necessary, be able to miss the odd hour's sleep.

Some of the jobs listed above may well be too much for any one man and the Secretary and the Clerk of the Course will probably need a team of helpers to whom they can delegate some of the work.

Running a trial is also something of a public relations exercise especially if you are using a large area of land, with sections on the property of various land-owners. You should always make a point of checking your route with the police and the local council, as well as gaining permission from land-owners. But good organisers, conscious of their public image, will go further than this. Each farmer, or other land-owner, will be visited by a responsible member of the club, who explains exactly what the trial involves, makes sure that any particular areas of the man's land which he wants to keep clear are put out of bounds to the riders. Go further, invite the farmer to the actual trial, give him a programme, and there's no reason why you shouldn't ask him to flag the competitors away at the start. If you are going to have to open his gates to let competitors through, detail a club member to ensure that the gate is firmly closed after each man has passed.

Careless, off-hand behaviour with land-owners has cost the trials game more sections than noise has done or is likely to do.

From the above it will be pretty clear that many club members are going to be involved with the organisation of the event and have specific jobs to do on the big day. In fact, some clubs make it a rule that none of their members are allowed to ride in their own trial — just to make sure that there is no labour force shortage.

I'm not advocating anything too drastic, but, if necessary, some form of rota system could be devised to ensure that everyone gets a share of the riding and the paperwork in their own club's promotions. One penalty I would advise for actual competing members of the organising club is that they must provide at least two observers before being allowed that privilege.

Make friends, too, with the local press. They are the ones who will project the image your event gives to the local population. And you want that image to be good. Drop a line to the Sports Editor well before the meeting, giving him an idea what the event involves, how many competitors from which areas are likely to take part, and inviting him and his photographer along to watch. Cultivate his interests on the day and make sure that he receives a copy of the programme and a set of results as soon as possible after the event.

When marking out sections try wherever possible to select natural hazards which do not need vast quantities of cards and, worst of all, tape. Some of the very best sections in use today simply have begins and ends cards and, although that sort of layout is the ultimate, remember that a competitor faced with a sea of markers or yards of tape is going to be put off the event before he gets into the section.

Sections should always be numbered consecutively from the start. In areas where a large number of sections are being squeezed into a small area of ground, it is sometimes difficult for a competitor to find his way around the course. The last thing he wants to do is miss a section and thereby lose marks or, depending on the regulations, risk exclusion. If the sections are clearly numbered on the begins cards, he can always backtrack to find the hazard he knows he has missed.

Ultra-long sections can, and should be, divided up into a series of sub-sections with an observer for each. It is not necessary to have neutral ground between each sub but be sure to put the cards marking the end of one sub from the beginning of the next on a fairly easy piece of terrain. This way there should be no difficulty in the observers deciding in which sub, if any, a competitor has lost marks.

Course marking

Various methods can be used to mark the course, the favourite in England being cards on trees, hedgerows etc. Three types of cards are used: white for straight on; blue for a left turn and red for a right. Cards should always be positioned well before a corner and not directly at the turn itself or you will have a potentially dangerous situation with riders making U-turns as they see the cards too late and others riding up behind them.

Some degree of commonsense must also be used in the siting of the cards. I have been to trials where red cards have been stuck on red postboxes, making them all but impossible to see.

The other difficulty with a course marked by cards is that there is, unfortunately, a certain element of the public, ill-disposed to the motorcycle fraternity, who will take a delight in removing or even changing around the cards you have so carefully displayed. These people, or even school kids having fun, can wreak havoc to the best designed route. The best answer here is to have one club member, who knows the route, armed with a collection of duplicate cards, riding around 10 minutes in front of the first competitor. Make sure all route markers are cleared away after the event as well as all litter.

Other methods of marking a route include dye on the roads, but this is a messy business in the extreme, can lead to friction with the local highways department and you're in big trouble, of course, if a strong wind blows up or it rains. One alternative, to which I'm not very partial, is to issue each rider with a route card at the start. Trouble is those riders who do not lose the card before they've gone five miles will finish up trying to ride along and read it at the same time — not in the greatest interest of road safety.

Competitors' numbers

Each rider should be provided with two numbers. One for the front of the machine and another which can be seen by an observer at the rear. The front number presents no difficulty as most machines have a square plate to which the number can be held by two rubber bands — probably cut by the rider from an old inner tube. With rear numbers the design of the machine does not allow for such straightforward fixing. Therefore the rider must carry the number on his person and this is, perhaps, best done by using a folded-over card, stapled at its edges and threaded over the competitor's belt.

The ultimate is a riding vest with numbers clearly marked which are issued to each rider at the start. Problem is that many competitors see these as souvenirs and the bibs you get back at the finish are likely to be considerably less in number than you started with. Sponsors often like to supply and endorse such bibs.

One way of obtaining bibs is to approach a sponsor who will get a little advertising out of the deal as well. This bib was provided by the Strongbow Cider Company. I'm guessing the wearer is a pretty good customer anyway

One way out of this could be to insist on the rider handing over his vest before you allow him to sign off at the finish of the trial, or charge a deposit on the bib when signing on.

Signing on before the trial and off at the finish should be made a compulsory part of the rider's obligation. It works for his benefit too, as it tells the organisers whether a man has failed to finish and may need picking up from far out on the route.

A club doesn't need a big mobile office to act as a signing-on and off point. The back of a station wagon will do

Observers

For your club's first event it would be wonderful to have a first-class team of fully-trained observers ready to detail the riders' performances on each section. You should be so lucky! What you are likely to get is a collection of Auntie Lils, who come along to watch their favourite nephew perform in the 'races' but who can fairly easily be pressed into service. And don't be put off by the fact that Aunt Lil isn't an experienced graduate of the observers school. She may make a couple of errors. So what? You're not running the final round of the world championship with £1,000 hanging on the drop of a foot.

Just take your Aunties to one side before the event starts and run through the scoring system with them. Show them in a section just how marks are lost and how to mark them on the score sheet. With the right encouragement Lil could turn into a real enthusiast out every weekend with her special gum boots, storm coat and sou'wester. One word of warning to riders. I've been embarrassed a couple of times when arriving, not in my best mood at a poorly laid out section, and have sounded off in my best cockney invective about the ancestry of the man responsible. On hearing a gentle 'tut, tut' from under a scarecrow assortment of foul-weather gear, I look closer to see everybody's favourite grandma is the observer.

It's the club's job to look after the observers. Ideally each would be provided with a tent, pre-packed picnic hamper, bottle of champagne, portable television and the like. In reality they will settle for a polythene bag to keep the score card dry, a couple of sharp pencils and a packet of chewing gum.

Bill's been observing for 53 years - and still keeps a sense of humour

It's quite possible that your trial will be over two or more laps and, if so, be sure that the backmarker riding around after the last competitor on lap one has a quick word with each observer to make sure that there are no problems and to decide, after consultation, whether it is necessary to alter the hazard.

One thing that Auntie Lil will probably not be able to take is arguments with riders and she should be told quite clearly that her word is law. An observer should always give the benefit of any doubt to the rider, but also be firm when he or she is sure of the facts. My club always finds that it is a good plan to include a note in the programme, ostensibly an instruction to observers saying that anyone arguing is liable to exclusion. I say ostensibly because it can also be seen by the riders themselves and can be taken as a gentle hint.

I know that even in the biggest trials mistakes do happen when observers, with the very best of intentions, mark a man down for a greater penalty than he, in fact, incurred. At one trial, rider after rider went through a particular section for the loss of three. Then along came a superstar, having the ride of his life, who got all the way through for just one mark. 'Three' said the observer. The official had been unintentionally brainwashing himself. Time and again he had seen riders lose three and in his mind he saw it yet again. In that case I was able to intervene and the rider got his fair score, but without a clearly unbiased witness he would have had little chance.

Such mistakes can, of course, cost a rider hundreds of pounds if the trial or title is lost as a result. But it's all a case of roundabouts and swings, and the real ace will always try to ride so well so as to win by such a margin that he can allow for the odd observer discrepancy.

Of course there will always be a bit of gamesmanship involved by riders towards observers and I've indulged in the sport myself. Funny thing is, one is less likely to get away with anything with Auntie Lil than one is with a seasoned official. All one can really ask of observers is that they are consistent.

One difficulty that a novice observer is likely to have is deciding whether a bike which comes to rest very near the ends cards has actually completed the section. The accepted rule is that the spindle of the front wheel is held to be the datum point. If the spindle passes the imaginary line between the ends cards then the bike has got through. This basically means that if a rider has been clean up to the ends card itself, he has still had a fault-free ride for the spindle must have already crossed the line. Even if the rider and machine come to an ungainly end, spread-eagled in the section, as long as the rider has not touched the ground before the spindle cleared the cards he still doesn't rate a failure.

No difficulty for rider or observer here. The ends cards are positioned on flat ground and few will argue whether a bike actually passes them or not

But what about this case? The bike has got almost over the climb before the front rears up. Question is, did the spindle pass the cards or not?

Not the perfect end to an attempt, but with the ends cards on the far right - there will be no argument as to whether the competitor reached the finish before going on his ear

Conversely, the bike has not entered the section until the front wheel spindle goes through. This is particularly important when sections are divided into two subs. Here it is important to have an observer who can see the imaginary line dividing the first sub-section from the second. Otherwise, it is possible for a rider who stops with his wheel spindle near the section dividing line to be debited five marks on each of the hazards by each observer, both of whom think the stop was in his own part of the course.

The observer's job is to note the performance of each rider, and this can be done by one of two basic methods. Scores for the complete entry can be kept by each observer or, alternatively, each rider can be given a card on which the result of his attempt on every section is recorded.

Of the two systems, the second is by far the best but it does have a few drawbacks. Its advantages are that the individual rider cards can speed results whereby, as each competitor arrives at the finish, his card can be taken, simply totted up and his performance seen. In a multi-lap event, running scores can go up on a board lap-by-lap, keeping the press, mechanics and a rider's family as well as the competitors themselves, informed on just how the event is progressing. This method also confirms the rider's performance on each section so he has immediate contact with the observer and can query — not argue — his marks.

But, as I said, the set-up has its disadvantages. Carrying a card around, trying to keep it dry — if it's not the plastic punch-hole variety — and worrying about its loss is aggravating to the rider who has got plenty enough to worry about. At least two officials are necessary for each section as one man must be at the exit to mark the card and the other at the optimum vantage point to judge performances. With the rider-carried cards, a card lost by the competitor must obviously mean the man's exclusion as the vital record of his performance would no longer be available.

Results

Whichever system is used for tabulating the performances, a team of clubmen is going to have a late night after the trial, working out the results. And I do mean a late night or even an early morning. For it is vital that those results get to the press and the competitors as soon as possible. Sorting out the results can be a sweat but you might as well have a complete nervous breakdown and be done with it.

Full results with as much detail as possible not only give the riders the assessment of their performances but also provide them with the chance to re-live the trial all over again — to compare their rides with those of their friends and rivals.

Back in the dark days when we had a very fast postal service in Britain, my club used to start work immediately after our event, sort the results, duplicate them, drive to the main post office in London and ensure that on the morning after the event the result sheets would drop through the front door of every rider's home.

Time limits

In recent years time limits have been set on some top trials to the events' considerable detriment. We are taking part in an artistic sport not a flat-out scramble. Obviously it is necessary to ensure that there is not too much hanging around and this can be achieved by giving observers the power to dock an automatic five marks if a rider refuses to attempt a section when called upon to do so. It's also possible to slot in a club member between every 50 or so riders. This man will ride around at a reasonable speed, allowing for inspection of sections and any delays. Any competitor passed by this official can be deemed to have been excluded from the event.

It's quite possible, especially during a club's first trial, that delays will occur. And, if you have found it expedient to set a time limit for each competitor, some provision must be made for a delay allowance. It is quite possible that weather conditions, suddenly worsening, will lead to a big backlog of riders attempting to climb a particular hill and here the observer should make a note of an official time allowance for the riders concerned. At the end of the trial this allowance can be added to the official time permitted and riders only penalised if they exceed the total.

Entries

When your club has published and distributed regulations for a trial, the entries will soon start flooding in. Beware, there are professional kings of the early or late number. Every area has its own local ace whose reputation is built up not on riding skill but his knowledge of the terrain over which each event is held and his speed, or tardiness, in sending in his entry. If the trial coming up is a super-muddy event Local Ace will get his entry in, delivered by hand perhaps, at the first possible moment, thus getting an early number and the advantage of being able to attempt each section before the ground is too cut up by the rest of the field. In a rocky event that same man will mysteriously get his entry in at the last possible minute so that the loose boulders get moved out of his way by the time he gets to the sections.

To stop this type of opportunism, a club should accept all entries up to a certain date or sooner if the number of riders fills up earlier. Officials should then ballot for starting order so that luck only decides whether one man should have any advantage over another.

If your trial includes a class for novices these should be balloted separately and sent off at the start of the entry. In this way they will get any possible advantage in a muddy event and move away any loose rocks in a boulder-strewn event so that the sections are as 'developed' as possible by the time the experts arrive.

For the all-important British Experts trial the organising club have a bevy of non-competitors go through the various sections before the riders arrive. This cuts down on any early-number advantage or disadvantage but can, obviously, only be used for the really big events where the number of officials and helpers is near unlimited.

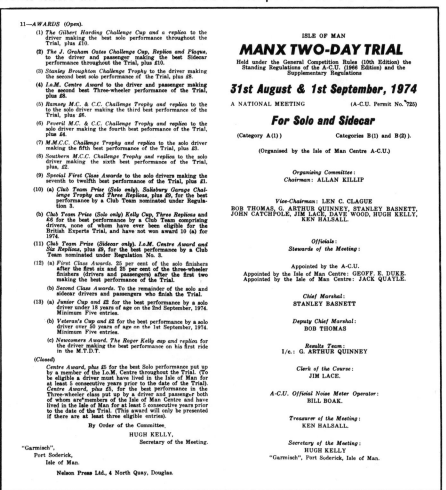

SUPPLEMENTARY REGULATIONS

1—*ANNOUNCEMENT.*

The I.o.M. Centre A-C.U. will hold a NATIONAL TWO-DAY TRIAL on Saturday, 31st AUGUST and Sunday, 1st SEPTEMBER, 1974 for Solo Motor Cycles and Sidecars under A-C.U. Permit No. 725. To be eligible to enter this meeting all drivers must be in possession of a current National or International Licence for Trials events issued by the A-C.U., the Scottish A-C.U. or M.C.U. of Ireland

The trial will be an observed trial of Two Days duration. The sections will be situated in groups at various points on the Island, and riders will be penalised for touching, footing and failure. The roads and tracks etc. between the groups of sections do not form part of the trial, although a route will be marked purely for the convenience of riders; but riders may follow any route they wish between groups of sections. The trial will start and finish at the Grandstand, Glencrutchery Road, Douglas, Isle of Man. There will be a short stop each day at approximately half distance where petrol and oil will be available and light refreshments will be provided. The meeting will be held under Standing Regulations (1974 Edition) and General Competition Rules (10th Edition) of the Auto Cycle Union and the following Supplementary Regulations:—

2—*ENTRIES.*

Entries will be accompanied by the appropriate fee of £4.25 for Solos and £5 for Sidecars (which includes light refreshments on each day of the trial, Personal Accident Insurance covering all drivers and passengers, and third party cover for private land only). The entries will not be accepted unless the form contains the whole of the information required. An entry form which does not show the driver's and/or entrant's 1974 National or International Competition Licence number shall be null and void. (G.C.R. No. 169). (10th edition). Entries will be limited to 210 solo and 30 sidecars, minimum for sidecars—20. Entry forms and regulations wll be posted on June 19th, on June 29th the organising committee will grade the entry, ballot for numbers, and inform applicants accepted, returning unsuccessful applicants entry fees. Priority will be given to competitors who have won first class awards or higher in National or International Trials, and to team entries. Ten solo and ten sidecar entries will be reserved for local riders qualified for the I.O.M. centre award. Entry fees will ONLY be returned to drivers in the event of postponement for more than 24 hours or abandonment. The Organising Committee reserves the right to refuse an entry without assigning any reason. Entries close on the 29th June, 1974. Should the minimum entry of 20 sidecars not be received, and the sidecar section cancelled, drivers will be informed immediately after 29th June, 1974.

3—*CLUB TEAMS (Solo and Sidecars).*

Team awards will only be awarded where there is a minimum number of three teams entered. Each team will consist of three drivers. Teams cannot be entered direct, but must be nominated from drivers already entered. A driver may not be nominated for more than one team. Teams must be nominated by the 31st July, accompanied by the entrance fee of £1. A team award will also be awarded to the highest placed solo team comprising drivers, none of whom have ever been eligible for the British Expert Trial, and who have not won award for 10(a) for 1974. Teams must be comprised of either all solo or all Sidecars. If one or more members of the team become non-starters, they may be replaced by other club riders who are entered in the Trial, but not entered in a team. Riders cannot be transferred from one team to another except from teams which are not complete due to non-starters, and when there are no other club members entered in the Trial.

4—*CHANGE OF DRIVER, PASSENGER OR MACHINE*

No change of driver and/or passenger or machine will be permitted unless application in writing is made to the Secretary of the Meeting before Saturday, 17th August, 1974. Change of driver may be permitted only if the driver was nominated by an entrant holding a 1974 Entrants National or International Competition Licence.

5—*SIGNING ON.*

Drivers must sign on and produce 1974 National or International Competition Licences before the Trial starts. The Trial H.Q., at the Grandstand, Glencrutchery Road, Douglas, will be open for this purpose and for the issue of route cards, final instructions, etc., between 7 p.m. and 9 p.m. on Thursday, 29th August and Friday, 30th August. Any driver failing to produce his National or International Competition Licence may only be permitted to start at the discretion of the Stewards of the Meeting and may be liable to a fine not exceeding £1.

6—*COURSE.*

Drivers must report with their machines between 7-30 a.m. and 9-15. a.m. on Saturday, 31st August, and Sunday, 1st September to the Control Officer at the Grandstand, Glencrutchery Road, Douglas, for presentation of machines to the Machine Examiner, who will be in attendance, and machines will not be removed from Control until moved to the starting line. Drivers will be despatched at 30 second intervals. Any driver not on the starting line at the correct time will be penalised one mark for every minute he is late in starting to a maximum of fifteen minutes after which time he will be deemed a non-starter. The Trial will start at 8-15 a.m. on both days. The course will be marked with direction cards, arrows and powder. Solo drivers will be started in reverse order on the Sunday, commencing with No. 211 at 8-15 a.m.

Riders must ensure that they have the correct vehicle licence on their machines. The vehicle licence must bear the same number as the Registration Number of the machine. Drivers must produce their current insurance certificate.

7—*ROUTE CARDS AND NUMBERS.*

Each Solo and Sidecar machine must be fitted at the driver's expense with one plate at the front, and one on either side securely fixed to the machine.

Number plates will be 6 ins. high by 8 ins. wide, painted black and the number will be allocated and notified by post. It will be the responsibility of the entrant to paint the allocated number thereon in white, so that the same are clearly legible. The side plates must be so fixed that they will not be obscured by either the driver or the passenger.

The driver will be issued with a Route Card for his convenience. The onus of finding the sections rests entirely on the driver. A Map of the course will be exhibited at Trial H.Q., Grandstand, Glencrutchery Road, Douglas.

The driver will be issued with a card giving the situation of each group of sections, and a suggested route to follow. A map showing the situation of all sections will be exhibited at Trial Headquarters, Grandstand, Glencrutchery Road, Douglas.

8—*TIMES OF ARRIVAL AT SECTION, ETC.*

(a) Drivers will be given a card for each day which will show time of arrival of the marshals at the various sections, and riders must ensure they do not arrive before these times.

(b) Drivers will be checked in and out of the short stop for petrol and light refreshments each day.

(c) Drivers must in all cases line up on the left side of the road. Straggling across the road is absolutely prohibited. Penalty —Exclusion.

9—*OBSERVED SECTIONS.*

in accordance with Standing Regulation No. 18 (1974 Edition), a failure will be deemed to have occurred when:

(a) The machine ceases to move in a forward direction relative to the **course.**

(b) The driver or passenger dismounts.

(c) Any wheel of the machine crosses an artificial boundary.

(d) The machine travels outside any boundary marker or if the driver or passenger is held responsible for breaking and/or removing a tape and/or support.

(e) The machine, the driver or passenger receives outside assistance.

(f) Any part of the passenger touches the ground.

Footing will be deemed to have occurred when any part of the body of the driver touches the ground. Penalty for Failure, 5 marks; touching the ground once only in a Section or Sub-Section, 1 mark; touching the ground twice, 2 marks; more than twice, 3 marks.

Drivers must be prepared to attempt a Section when called upon to do so by an official. Penalty for non-compliance 5 marks which is additional to any penalty which may subsequently be incurred in the section concerned.

10—*TIES.*

Ties will be decided as follows:—

(a) The rider with the greatest number of sections cleaned.

(b) The rider who has gone the furthest with no loss of marks.

These methods of deciding ties will only apply to awards (1) to (12f). All ties between first and second class award winners will be shown as ties.

Awards

When I was a schoolboy, I was making a delivery to the house of a local rider when I glimpsed, through an open door, a trophy cabinet bulging with cups, tankards and other tangible evidence of his prowess. I'll admit it. I was green with envy. Up until then all that interested me was the thought of riding bikes but the sight of all that hardware was a further incentive to that impressionable youngster.

Well, I got them. At first I had enough to put on the top of the television, then they graduated to the sideboard. More came and my own cabinets went up first on one wall and then on others. Soon there were cups and trophies all over the house.

Want to know where they are now? Stacked in cardboard boxes in the attic. That's where.

I'll admit that I've got beyond the point where a cup means anything and nowadays I don't even bother to take those which have to be returned a year later out of their boxes. But I do remember the early years and how much those awards meant to me and therefore I strongly advocate giving trophies. Some clubs give cash prizes, others use book vouchers and I suppose we're not far off the gift-stamp trial. But it'll be a sad day for everyone but the superstar, and even he, if pushed, will admit that no cash or kind could replace his trophies — even if they are mouldering in the loft.

I suggest that a club gives awards for the first, second and third in the expert class and for first in the novice and intermediate categories. Add first-class awards for the best 10 per cent in each class and second-class awards for the next 10 per cent.

Machine examination

As each rider signs on at the start of the event a knowledgeable individual should check over the bike to ensure that it is in a safe condition. Clearly, slightly dodgy brakes could be overlooked for an event in a closed-to-traffic sand pit or confined to a wood. But the same brakes could constitute a danger if the trials sections are linked by long stretches of public road. Machine examination is all a matter of commonsense.

The same argument goes for the problem of noise. It's really a question of degree and of responsibility to the public. Talk of specific decibel figures drives me mad. If you shut this book quickly — don't, you'll lose your place — the noise would be something like 90 decibels, enough to have a bike excluded in some events.

There used to be an old adage that a noisy bike was a fast bike. There may even have been some truth in it when the big four-stroke ruled the trials roost, but today a man who modifies his exhaust system in an attempt to release full power is simply doing his fellow competitors a favour. At Kawasaki, it takes a multi-million dollar computer and a team of top-notch experts to design the exhaust system on a trials machine. They are aiming to produce a low-level of noise but also to provide the necessary expansion volume and exhaust outlet diameters which allow a two-stroke engine to develop its power. The man who does his tuning with a hacksaw and produces an ear-shattering, anti-social din, has also, probably, altered the power characteristics of his engine considerably.

In national trials in England noise meters are already part of the scene. These are sited, usually on steep climbs where the engine is working hard and any excessive noise likely to be clearly evident. The penalty for exceeding the permissible decibel rating is 10 marks — the equivalent of failing two sections more than the man with a quieter exhaust system.

And I'm not knocking the noise meter. To me a trials machine is a quiet, friendly machine incapable of annoying even the most reactionary conservationist.

Those who delight in making a din, do our sport no service at all, and there is much to be said for the American Motorcycle Association's maxim *Less sound, more ground*. For we motorcyclists can give the anti-bike brigade who are trying to drive out sport from the open spaces no greater weapon than the cry of excessive noise.

12
Ride a trial with me

It's 4.30 on a Saturday afternoon. I'm riding in a small local trial tomorrow and, believe it or not, I'm getting nervous.

It's not a big event. Simply open to riders in the 34 clubs that form the Eastern Centre of the British A-CU. Yet it's going to be a difficult trial to win, because the sections are likely to be too easy.

Opposition tomorrow will be the local aces. They'll know the ground like their own window-boxes and, anywhere in the world, a man riding on his own doorstep is hard to beat.

They'll be out to beat me. Topping a factory development engineer on a new, prototype bike would be a great feather in their caps. That gives them — and there are at least eight who could pull off a win — that little extra determination which makes all the difference.

Still I've got something going for me. I know they're good riders but I don't think any of them is quite up to my standard. But the only thing I've got to spur me on is the thought of the pain of being beaten by someone who is less experienced.

Were this a big National event, or an International, I would have no qualms about heading riders of tomorrow's calibre in the results. But, the great problem is that I will only have to make one silly mistake and the trial will be lost. With super-tough, national-type sections there's always a chance for a rider to pull back with an ace ride and atone for a silly five elsewhere. Tomorrow there will be no chance. I know the answer is to not make an error. But there are eight of them. Only one of me. The odds aren't on my side.

The thought's getting me down. I'm already becoming edgy and short-tempered. Nothing for it but to wheel out my 900 cc Kawasaki roadster and blow away some hang-ups.

This is where the fun goes out of my sport or, I suppose, any sport. I spent years winning such trials and then I had no pre-event worries. I would have been certain I was going to win — now I'm not so sure. There are three reasons: I think that the other riders now believe that they can beat me and I have lost the psychological edge I had before; what is worse, I believe now that I can be beaten; my mental approach has changed. My main aim is not now focussed on trying to win but in developing the ultimate in trials machines and promoting the sport.

I'm now in a state of mind where I demand of myself that I win. That can be a big problem for, when a rider reaches this stage and the pressure becomes continuous he must decide whether he still enjoys trials overall. If not, he should get out. Thank God I still do enjoy the trials game even if I am moving into the twilight as a top-class competitor.

I must get a grip of myself. Tomorrow morning I will be quiet, curt and frightfully efficient. I'll expect my favourite breakfast, perfectly cooked and set on the table exactly on time. I'll then be able to leave in plenty of time allowing for any hold-ups on route and not getting frustrated with the antics of Sunday morning drivers. The trial is only about an hour away and I'm glad. Anything over a two-hour trip and I would probably be leaving this evening to stay overnight near the start. You can expend a lot of nervous energy just getting to an event. And I, like anyone else, have only got so much.

At least the bike is mechanically perfect, but it's a bit dusty from a spot of midweek

practice. The fact that it's not super-clean is troubling me a little as I normally like to turn up with an immaculate machine. Mind you, I could even get a psychological advantage over the other riders if they see that I have been out practising. Oh dear. I've just remembered being blown off in a similar event late last year. I'll have to rectify that tomorrow — and that means stop worrying right now.

It's Sunday morning. I've just had eggs, bacon, four slices of bread and probably double the amount of marmalade that anyone else would use. The sun's shining and although photographer Graham Forsdyke, who is in the car with me, is enthusing about the light available for his pictures, I would have preferred a more miserable day.

I used to get a kick out of super weather, but then realised that everyone else was doing the same. With quite a bit of effort I managed to school myself into knowing that I could ride as well in really dirty conditions which would put the other riders off. Again I was looking for that psychological advantage.

We arrive. The trial is just how I pictured it. Ten sections to be completed three times and all in an area not much bigger than a football stadium. It's good for mum and the kids. They can watch dad perform on practically every section and already I see deck chairs and picnic stoves being set up on the hillside.

I sign on, am given my number and await my time to be off. The first three sections are less than 50 yards away. So I use the minutes until my time comes up in having a look at the opening hazards. I like the first section. The Clerk of the Course obviously knew what he was about. It's fairly easy and no one with start-of-trial nerves is going to do himself mischief.

The second section is giving a little trouble to the early numbers already as it includes a sharp rise out of a stream onto the bank. Water is being brought up the bank and a large hole is developing just before it. Can't think why all the riders are going through the hole. When I come to inspect the section in detail I'll explore to the right and left.

The third section is similar, except that the exit, up another river bank, is already beginning to look very ugly. There's a muddy morass at that point. I would want to accelerate up and out and it could be that the best way to tackle it would be to rely on speed to conquer the mud, with sufficient left over to carry me on up the bank.

It's getting near time to officially start and at last I'm flagged away. As I expected the first section creates no problems. Whilst I am waiting in the queue for the second hazard, riders are trying both to the left and right of the line I had decided to avoid. I opt for the left hand choice and again I am clean.

Last job before the off. Tyre pressures depend very much on weather conditions so make sure you check them before the starters flag goes down

That ugly mud on the exit to the third section has got worse, and I spend quite a bit of time stomping through it trying to decide whether the wheels will cut through the goo and provide grip for the climb. This could be just the section that decides the trial.

A nod from the observer, second gear engaged, a few moments' concentration and I am off. The first part of the section was easy, but now I'm facing the climb out, and accelerate towards it. The bank is a lot more slippery than I imagined and down goes my right foot to steady the plot at the top.

Well, that's the first mark cast away. I could probably have got away without it, but it's early on in the trial and I'm playing a little cautious.

Section four is a collection of tight turns and a slight climb up a camber. It's all a question of whether to use first or second gear. I decide that machine positioning is going to be all-important and therefore, wanting to go as slowly as possible, I'll opt for the lower ratio. The rider in front of me does the same and stalls the bike on the second turn. Was that him or the result of using first gear. Damn it, I'll stick to my plan. The observer nods, I select the gear and a voice in my ear says: *hello Don, how are things going?* It's an old friend. I like him a lot. But I need idle chit-chat at this moment like I need a hole in my head. I can't be rude. We chin-wag for a few minutes and he backs off and I start the mental approach thing over again. Into the section, around the turns, across the camber and through the ends card; no problems. First gear was right. I'll use it again on laps two and three.

Hello, we are going to do some mountain climbing. The fifth section has a super-steep climb and I bet when I walk to the top there'll be a tight turn ready to catch out the man who had too much speed on the incline.

I'm right. The course goes sharp left and, if I'm going to go with it, I'll need to arrive at the top at exactly the right speed — practically stationary. Again I'm not sure which gear to use. Only this time it's a choice between second and third. Third will make the climb much easier but then I'll need to change down at the top — just when I want to be concentrating on that tight turn. The only problem with second is that if I approach too fast the bike will run out of revs halfway up the hill. I'll be here all day if I don't get a grip and, Graham is fidgeting. He's focussed both cameras three times already and is digging so deep into our sandwich supply that there won't be any left unless I get to them soon.

OK, I'll use second. But to ensure that the bike does not run out of revs halfway up I'll take a much shorter run than the others are doing; and drive the bike all the way to the top.

I'm guessing right today — again no problem.

The sixth section is practically number five in reverse and presents no problems. Onto section seven which is an easy run along the side of a hill but with one fierce camber just before the ends card. The bike is going to have to be positioned just right and I shall need to get speed on so that I can float up the camber steadily. That camber's so fierce that if I twitch an eyelid while the bike's on it, one wheel or the other will drop down.

I'm through but only just. I made a big error and underestimated the severity of a hump just before the camber. It threw me much higher up the hill than I wanted. My front wheel went on full lock and had it not been for the fact that everything else was right it would have been a five and any chance of winning the trial right down the drain.

At last another section without any problems. Number eight is a first-gear wobble, and I was brought up on first-gear wobbles.

The next hazard is just about the same except that the initial climb has a small hump on the approach and I'm careful not to launch myself off it or I will hit the incline with as much weight as a bag of bricks.

I'm still smarting from the thought that I could have got away from the dab on section three when a friendly observer tells me that one of the local aces has lost two fives in the first four sections. The last hazard of the first lap gets us mixed up with the only trees in the trial. But the foliage is not the problem. The sweat comes with a short, but steep, downhill drop and a very wicked, tight U-turn back up the hill again. I'll be wanting to come down so slow you'll

Here's an eagle-eyed observer ready to dock me marks if I slide down the banking and into the section marking. He's also well-equipped and the stake in front of him has obviously given many riders trouble as he has a mallet ready to replace it

Descent technique. Correct balance and lining up is all-important

Another descent. I'm practically at a standstill ensuring that I have the minimum speed to scrub off on the drop

With the correct speed, machine positioning and angle of approach short, sharp banks, even out of rivers, cause no difficulty

Further down and the brakes are working hard

End of lap one and a breather before the next circuit

hardly know I'm moving.

Top of the hill ready for the descent. Ease the bike down and, oh God, no front brake. The linings must have got wet in section three. You'd think I'd have learned about drying out brakes by now. I grab the front brake lever and give it all the pressure I've got but I'm still coming down like a Swiss avalanche. At the bottom the damn brake dries out and grabs. The sudden wrench almost slings me over the bars and that graceful U-turn I had envisaged turns into a desperate dab which only just pulls me out of trouble.

That's the first lap over and I'm two marks down. Not good enough, Smith. You're not going to have the trial away, riding like that. Remember to ask each observer whether, even easy sections, have been altered for the second circuit.

No need to make any enquiries for section one. Someone thought it was too easy and has introduced a nasty kink at the start. But I discover a line through and am all ready to use it when I notice a loose boulder right where my front wheel needs to go. A pal reads my mind and says, *you want me to wander through and kick that away don't you Don?* But before I can *yes* the observer calls me yet again. And, rather than hold up the trial, I have to make my move.

I'm not going to risk the front wheel rolling off the rock — and try to get round it. The bike gets off-line and another mark goes on my score.

Had this been a big event with bonus money riding on it, I would probably have turned a deaf ear to the observer and waved someone else on ahead of me, or had a little instant machine trouble. But what the hell!

Section two again. Someone's really been getting at the hazards. Now they want us to whistle in and out of the stream three times, but it's still no sweat.

No one has dared to do anything to worsen section three, where I lost my first mark on lap one. It's got worse by itself. The bank has been cut away more by desperately spinning rear wheels. And the earth has simply fallen to increase the mass of mud below. Still, let's make amends. The easy bit's just as easy and I approach the problem quite confidently.

Oh hell. That mud grabs hold of the back wheel and it's like I've thrown an anchor out. The bike makes it to the top but only just and the front wheel rears up and away, floating over the ends card. Blast — that's really done it. The observer's quite a way away and it's anyone's guess whether she thought the wheel went inside or outside the card. That's how trials are lost. I feel sick. I misjudged it. A little more speed and it would have been no problem. Even had I got in trouble I could have got away with a dab. If that was five I guess I'm out of the race.

I carry on. But unless I'm careful I'm going to lose concentration. I could still win, but I don't fancy my chances. Still I'll go down fighting. And that means not losing another mark.

It was a turning point in my career when, as a youngster, I was given some important advice by a then superstar. Triumph factory rider Roy Peplow took me to one side after witnessing my considerably less than perfect display on one section. He told me never to give up and that no trial is ever won or lost until the last hazard has been completed. Roy was right and it's advice I've passed on to countless riders ever since.

This time I'm very careful on section ten and dry my brakes out thoroughly beforehand. The section's no trouble and I end the second lap with a total of either three or eight marks against my name.

Now I'm determined to complete the last lap clean. And that means section three as well which has cost me marks on both previous tours. When I get to what may have been my Waterloo it's as bad as ever. But suddenly I see a new set of tyre tracks. Instead of climbing out through the morass, they sneak along the river bank, climb out at a much easier spot, and edge the bike back to the ends card — looping, certainly not playing the game and, in fact, illegal. I'm standing at the section, worrying whether the observer will let riders get away with it, when I notice that a local ace has seen the line as well. He discusses it with a couple of riders and the three of them decide to give it a try. The first goes through and it's like a main road to him, but he collects a few boos from the crowd. The observer is flummoxed. She doesn't know what to give him. Soon there's a gaggle of riders around her demanding to know whether the ride was legal. For, if she gives way, we will all avoid the trouble spot. Hello, she's got up. She's walking away. Our observer has either gone on strike or is off to seek advice from an official. We all stand around pondering until she returns.

She makes a decision. *Through the morass or its five.*

Well, that's sorted that out. Got to save a little face, and I do. With the little more speed that I should have used on lap two, the bike fights its way through the mud and sails out between the ends cards.

I get a clap but that's poor consolation for the five I threw away on the previous circuit.

I achieve my ambition of finishing without losing any more marks and now must wait for the club to publish the results.

The organisers were quite snappy in doing their deliberations and the same night I hear that the observer on dreaded number three section did, indeed, decide my front wheel had gone outside the marker. And, as I feared, a couple of other competitors had got round with less marks than my total. Ah well, you can't win 'em all.

An easy drop into a stream bed. Here correct speed, positioning and a correct gear selected will pay dividends

The beginning of the end. The dreaded third section and I'm about to lose five marks. The bike is desparately clawing for grip and about to suddenly find too much. Already the front wheel is running too light and a split second later it slewed round over the ends card

The third section of the last lap. This time I had speed well calculated and came out of it clean

A simple drop into a pond, but positioning is important for the short, sharp climb to come

WORLD TRIALS CHAMPIONSHIP BUILD-UP

1964—1965	Don Smith	Greeves
1965—1966	Gustave Franke	Zundapp
1966—1967	Don Smith	Greeves
1967—1968	Sammy Miller	Bultaco
1968—1969	Don Smith	Montesa
1969—1970	Sammy Miller	Bultaco
1970—1971	Mick Andrews	Ossa
1971—1972	Mick Andrews	Ossa
1972—1973	Martin Lampkin	Bultaco
1974—1975	Malcolm Rathmell	Bultaco

13
World trials championship

It took 13 years' hard work before the Federation Internationale Motorcycliste — governing body of all motorcycle sport — recognised trials sufficiently to grant the sport world championship status.

I first started riding on the Continent back in 1961 and reckon now to know every ship's captain, purser and bar boy by name. In those dark days, trials were barely tolerated by the FIM and it certainly wasn't any official encouragement that put trials on the map. The only reason we now have a world championship is because of the basic enthusiasm of a handful of people on both sides of the English Channel.

Back in 1961 the standard of riding on the Continent was low — about British Open-to-Centre standard today. Trials were held in Holland, Germany and Belgium and I used to try to get Greeves to send me to as many of them as possible.

OK, I enjoy foreign travel, meeting new people, seeing new places and I'm not adverse to the wild parties that sometimes follow the events, but my main reason for the trips was to promote the sport in countries which had seldom before seen proficient riders. Even then, I saw the possibility of a European and a World title emerging.

The first move towards any recognition was in late 1962 when the Belgians, who had been pestering the FIM, pushed through an international contest to be decided over a number of trials, on a team basis.

Because it's always more difficult for the public to appreciate a team performance, rather than a solo effort, the contest did not set the World alight. In fact, it got a very luke-warm reception from both public and press alike.

But it was something — not much, but something. Although it was a little disheartening to drive down to Dover, catch a midnight boat to Holland or France, ride your heart out, perhaps even win and then see only a terse paragraph in the press, we knew that the ball was finally rolling.

The great, great thrill came in Belgium late in 1963. As the riders gathered in the local club-house for a final beer before turning in for the night, the news came through. First as a whispered rumour, then as a confirmed roar. A telegram had arrived from the FIM's headquarters in Geneva that the next day's event would count towards a new individual title.

Still it was not to be called a European Championship but the Henri Groutars Prize. Groutars, a Belgian, was one of the greatest names in the Continental trials game. So great was his enthusiasm that during the Second World War he ran trials, with ten men to one machine, under the noses of the Germans — with petrol, liberated from Nazi fuel dumps.

You can imagine my enthusiasm when I got the news — and how hard I tried the next day. Although the FIM had hung the name Groutars on the contest it wasn't long before riders, press and public talked of it as a European Championship. It finally got that title in 1967 and then, strangely enough, the same men who had insisted on calling it a European Championship before, started talking of it as a World series.

And not without justification. In the early days of the Groutars events, only a few tradition-ally trials-minded countries ran rounds. But now we have 14 nations staging events including even Iron Curtain Czechoslovakia and Poland.

It's odd how long it takes the FIM to get a message. In 1974 when America entered the list of countries promoting events, the championship still wasn't given official world status. That was promised in 1974 for the '75 battle.

A look through the award winners reveals a near monopoly by British riders. Sammy Miller and Mick Andrews both have two championship wins, I have three. Only in 1965-66 did a non-Briton come out on top when Bavarian Gustave Franke headed the list. Now things have changed. From the very early days, foreign federations realised that British riders were supreme at trials and the enlightened officials organised training schools for their riders with Englishmen acting as tutors.

Of course, this did not pay off overnight but the improvement, although gradual, has certainly been steady. I can remember, in 1969, a schoolboy enthusiast haunting our depot at the Peugeot Hotel in Montbeliard. That young enthusiast was Charles Coutard. He's now the Trials Champion of France.

The Championship Series has been used by the three Spanish factories, Montesa, Ossa and Bultaco as proving grounds for their models. In fact, the Spanish learnt about trials from these international contests which may well explain why, even today, sections in Spanish-organised events rate as some of the hardest in the world.

Even as late as the start of the 1970s a win by a non-Englishman would be headline news. Now it's a distinct possibility.

Britain's pride almost suffered its most humbling blow in Wales in early 1974. Following the Spanish round, in which a virtually unknown Swede, fiery Ulf Karlsson had a runaway victory, English riders were ready to show the world that it must have been a fluke and that they still had an unshakable grip on the trials game.

And it all, very nearly, went wrong. Another foreigner, this time a Finn, Yrjo Vesterinen, lead the event from the start until very nearly the finish. Only a masterly ride by Yorkshireman Malcolm Rathmell saved the day for Britain on the very last section.

There are plenty of others quite capable of taking premier awards and Sweden seems to have more than its fair share. As well as Karlsson, they boast Benny Sellman, and quiet-spoken blond Thore Evertson.

As the title has developed in importance so it has graduated into a big-money deal for the riders.

Most factories run a works team of three men which, when only the trio of Spanish manufacturers were interested, meant a force of nine sponsored men. Now four Japanese factories — Suzuki, Honda, Yamaha and Kawasaki are entering the fray which brings the total number of superstars necessary up to a staggering 21 plus the up-and-coming men sponsored by factories with an eye to the future. These men are in big demand. In the late 1960's a top rider who had a good year could expect to earn around £500 for his labours. Now, if he wanted, the same man could rest for a year on the proceeds of the previous 12 months.

But all the money in the world isn't going to manufacture supermen out of average riders. There is going to be a great world shortage of top class men and when they do arrive I foresee many of them coming from America.

In the sports-orientated United States there are sufficient young men with enough cash-in-hand to take them through the first three years when a man is earning little but simply gaining the all-important experience. Any man with sufficient inclination and intelligence can be taught the tricks of the trade. No one can hand over experience.

14
The Scottish Six Days Trial

The Seventies may well be the boom decade for trials, but few of the newly-instituted events will ever get near the glamour and aura of the sport's greatest classic — The Scottish Six Days Trial — held annually in the Western Highlands.

The Scottish is what trials is all about. With only a break between 1939 and 1947 the trial, toughest and longest in the calendar, has attracted the best riders in the world. In the early years it was a complicated team event with three-man factory teams. I say three-man teams but in 1925, fourteen years after the event was first run, the award for the 350 cc class went to a Raleigh trio which included Miss Marjorie Cottle — most famous of all women riders.

In 1928 individual performances were recognised, but only in various capacity classes and without an overall winner. This was all very well and, perhaps, led to more factory support as there were increased chances of coming away with some form of award, but the public likes to see a winner. A man who stands out head-and-shoulders above his fellow competitors. And in 1932 the present award system with one overall winner was introduced.

Actually between 1932 and 1948 and in 1950 there were two winners each year, for a sidecar class was included.

Although always very popular with spectators, the trial and ability of solo machines soon outgrew those of the three wheelers. Nowadays sections have to be so tough to test the highly-developed skills of the riders and their ultra-competitive machinery that sidecars would have difficulty in getting even to the begins card on some of the hazards, and the crossing of Blackwater would be near impossible.

The list of solo winners in the Scottish reads like a trials world's Who's Who. The great Hugh Viney took an AJS to victory four times including a hat-trick in the first three post-war events. John Brittain gave Royal Enfield two successes and Jeff Smith — Britain's only Motocross World Champion — won in 1955. Gordon Jackson, now one of Britain's top trials car drivers, has equalled Hugh Viney's four wins. But the record stands at the moment to legendary Irish wizard Sammy Miller. Sammy won on his big 500 Ariel in 1962 and 1964 and then followed it up by putting Bultaco on the map the next year. His hat-trick attempt was foiled in 1966 by Alan Lampkin, brother of Arthur Lampkin who split Miller's run of victories with a win in 1963. Miller scored again in 1967 and 1968 to give him a total of five wins.

Now the only immediate challenger to Miller's record is quiet-spoken Derbyshire professional Mick Andrews who notched a hat-trick in 1970—72 on Ossa machines, lost out in a needle contest to Malcolm Rathmell the following year, but then came back in 1974 on a Yamaha to give Japan their first Scottish win.

The Scottish is the one big trial that always eluded me. I usually finished in the first handful, but that all-important win that would have meant so much never came my way. My first Scottish was in 1961 when I won the much prized award for the best newcomer. That year Gordon Jackson got around the six-day course with the loss of only one mark.

In my first drive I lost only 32, and I can remember thinking at the time how foolish it was that a classic event should have such easy sections. To lose only one, Gordon could not have been fully tested throughout the week and at that time I was losing more than 32 in winning little open-to-centre trials at home. The organisers in Edinburgh and District Motor Club obviously thought the same and slowly increased the severity of the sections until today we have gone the full route — from the sublime to the ridiculous.

Remembering that the organisers bill the event as a 'Clubman's holiday in the Highlands', some sections are far too severe. The winner of the best newcomer in 1974 was Finn Yjro Vesterinen. He was a top contender for the European Championship, had all but won the British round two months earlier and yet could only force his way through the Scottish rockery for a total penalty of 122. In the same year winner Mick Andrews went down for 41. Somewhere between the 1961 main-road jaunt and the 1974 event which for any clubman was just plain hard work, must be a mean. I would like to see the event transformed to have fewer near-impossible sections — just enough to test factory men to their maximum, but not so many as to put off the Highland holiday rider for all time.

The Scottish, with its near-800 miles of road and rough riding and its 160 sections is unique. I rate it with the TT, Daytona and the International Six Days Trial as one of the four greatest competitions in the Motorcycle calendar. Unfortunately, some of its glory seems to be disappearing. There was a time when a rider's entry fee included his accommodation — and free fuel was supplied. But, in the past few years, entry fees have risen and yet riders have now to sort out and pay for their own accommodation and petrol.

1974 was the worst yet. Not only did route marking seem to deteriorate but competitors were required for the first time to supply their own riding numbers. The year 1974 was probably that of my last Scottish performance. Had it been my first-ever event I would have probably got lost a couple of times and felt that perhaps the entry fee was exorbitant.

I'm not complaining for the sake of it. The Scottish is the greatest event in the calendar and I want it to remain just that.

Because of the event's prestige there is growing a number of similar events throughout the world. There's already a three-day event in Spain, and talk of similar competitions in America. But it's unlikely that they will interest the same riders, for in Scotland 90 per cent of the competitors are privateers who scrimp and scrape all the year for their holiday. Men go without beer and cigarettes; wives without a new washing machine and houses without a new coat of paint — just so that one man can ride in the SSDT.

Such is the lure of the Scottish.

Newer, multi-day events are likely to be much more dominated by factory riders. But if these competitions are to succeed, organisers must realise that it costs a factory an enormous amount of time and money to field the team in such a long international contest. This is a case where just having one winner is not enough. The factory's publicity men must have successes with which to advertise their products. And the more awards you give, the better their chances.

What I have said about the difficulty of the Scottish, the toughness of the terrain and the problems of the super-tough sections should not deter anyone from competing in this classic. With a machine that is 100 per cent fit at the start he will be able to get to the finish. If he is of only average ability it may well be that he has less time than the works aces to inspect the sections and less chance to continually alter his tyre pressures before and after each section. But he will still have a fantastic holiday and return to tell his friends and workmates of the mist-shrouded horizons, the snow on the mountains, the seemingly endless peat bogs, and the long lonely fighting against the clock over the terrors of Blackwater and Rannoch Moor. And he will be proud — for he has competed in the world's greatest trial.

Although the Scottish Six Days got under way in 1925 it was, for the first seven years, either a team event or one where class wins were rated more than the overall best performer.

In 1932 the award as we know it today came into force.

1932	R. Macgregor	Rudge
1933	L. Heath	Ariel
1934	J. Williams	Norton
1935	R. Macgregor	Rudge
1936	W.T. Tiffen	Velocette
1937	J. Williams	Norton
1938	G.F. Povey	Ariel
1939	A. Jefferies	Triumph
1947	B.H.M. Viney	AJS
1948	B.H.M. Viney	AJS
1949	B.H.M. Viney	AJS
1950	L.A. Ratcliffe	Matchless
1951	G.J. Draper	BSA
1952	J.V. Brittain	Royal Enfield
1953	B.H.M. Viney	AJS
1954	L.A. Ratcliffe	Matchless
1955	J.V. Smith	BSA
1956	G.L. Jackson	AJS
1957	J.V. Brittain	Royal Enfield
1958	G.L. Jackson	AJS
1959	R. Peplow	Triumph
1960	G.L. Jackson	AJS
1961	G.L. Jackson	AJS
1962	S.H. Miller	Ariel
1963	A.J. Lampkin	BSA
1964	S.H. Miller	Ariel
1965	S.H. Miller	Bultaco
1966	A.R.C. Lampkin	BSA
1967	S.H. Miller	Bultaco
1968	S.H. Miller	Bultaco
1969	W. Wilkinson	Greeves
1970	M. Andrews	Ossa
1971	M. Andrews	Ossa
1972	M. Andrews	Ossa
1973	M. Rathmell	Bultaco
1974	M. Andrews	Yamaha

Trials terminology

ACE — Top rider.

AMA — American Motorcycle Association, national sanctioning organisation.

BACK MARKER — A member of a promoting club who leaves the start of a trials event after the last competitor has started. He proceeds around the course and will assist any rider in trouble. He is an experienced mechanic and trials rider. His job is to see that the event keeps moving.
Any rider passed by the Back Marker is retired from the event. The Back Marker will inform each observer that a section is closed upon his passage through it. He will sometimes collect observers, score cards or will ask observers to return all their section markers and cards to the finish line.

BAJA — Lower California, Mexico, annual 500, 1,000 mile endurance runs.

BAULK — Competitor being interfered with by a spectator, another competitor or officials during his attempt on a section. Claimed at the time of incident, and 're-run' at the discretion of the observer.

BEGINS — Two large cards denoting the start of an observed section.

BELT — Rear chain.

BINDERS — Brakes.

BLADDERS — Trials tyre inner tubes ('flashing a bladder' — to change a tube).

BOONIES — An isolated riding area.

BOOTS — Trials tyres.

BORE — Cylinder diameter.

BORED — An engine increased in size by enlarging cylinders and pistons.

CANDLE — Spark plug.

C.D.I. — Capacitor Discharge Ignition.

CLEAN — Passage through whole section losing zero points (marks).

COLOURS — Term signifying racing colours such as Kawasaki team riders in green and white.

CONTINGENCY AWARD — Motorcycle, parts, and accessory manufacturers offer prizes in addition to purse money, for winning or placing riders using

their product.

DAB — See ONE.

ENDS — Two large cards denoting the finish of an observed section.

ENDURO — The name given to dirt and street motorcycles, racing with varying times and speeds.

EXPANSION CHAMBER — A specially-designed exhaust pipe for two-stroke engines.

F.I.M. — Federation Internationale Motorcycliste, international sanctioning organisation.

FIVE — Stopping or falling in an observed section losing 5 points or marks.

FORK BOOTS — A rubber fitting used to keep dirt out of front forks.

FORK BRACE — A heavy aluminium brace designed to keep forks in line under hard use.

FRAME — The basic assembly of a motorcycle without wheels, engine or fairing.

GATE — Pair of cards, markers or stakes between which rider must pass.

GET OFF — An abrupt, unplanned departure from the seat of a motorcycle.

I.S.D.T. — International Six Day Trials, annual international enduro — 'Olympics of Motorcycling'.

KIDNEY BELT — Worn by many professionals to prevent internal injuries caused by vibration or jarring.

KNOBBIES or KNOBBLIES — Special tyre with large rubber cleats providing excellent traction on dirt.

LINE — The passage chosen by an individual competitor as his best means of 'cleaning' a section without losing points.

LOOPING — Derived from 'loophole' or cheating. Turning out between two markers to enable straighter run at obstacle. Observer can mark 5. Some newcomers may try this procedure within the confines of a section which is allowed providing they do not cross their own wheel tracks — penalty 5 marks.

MIC — Motorcycle Industry Council.

NOVICE CLASS — Beginning division of motorcycling competition.

OBSERVER — Official who notes marks lost by rider

through various 'sections'.

ON THE PIPE — An engine running at peak power.

ONE — or 'Dab' or 'Prod' — using one foot once, losing 1 mark.

OVERSQUARE — An engine with its bore larger than its stroke.

PINGING — Engine clatter caused by pre-ignition or low octane fuel.

POWER BAND — Efficiency range of engine.

PROTEST — Letter of complaint forwarded to competition officials after the publication of event results. A fee is normally required which is usually returned if the protest is upheld either by the Stewards of the Meeting or a subsequent Court of Enquiry.

RABBIT — Very inexperienced rider-novice.

RE-RUN — As described with 'Baulk' and must begin at the observers discretion in an area prior to the baulk occurring. Marks lost by the competitor on his first attempt up to the point of baulk will be those recorded for the Official Results.

RIM LOCK — Keeps tyre from rotating on rim. (Security bolt)

ROCK GUARD — Protection for outer parts of crankcases.

RPM — Revolutions Per Minute of engine crankshaft.

SECTION — Parts of course where rider attempts to pass through 'clean'.

SEIZE — An engine lock up.

SHROUDS — Dust protectors for levers.

SIGNING ON/OFF — The signing of a sheet at the start of the Trials event. Failure to sign off infers the competitor has retired from the event and he is not classified in the official results.

SKID PLATE — Protective metal plate under the engine to prevent damage from rocks.

SKINS — Tyres or leather clothing.

SLOT — Groove worn in muddy section which becomes virtually the only line.

STINGER — Rear portion of expansion chamber.

STOCK BIKE — A motorcycle with minimal modifications. May or may not be street legal. Most often found in drag racing and enduros.

STREET BIKE — Usually a street-legal motorcycle with no modifications.

STROKE — Distance piston travels.

SUB — One complete section of a number of continuous sections.

SWING ARM — Rear suspension arm.

THREE — Also known as 'footing' — using feet more than twice losing 3 marks.

THUMPER — Single cylinder four-stroke motorcycle.

TICKLE — The deliberate priming of an engine to facilitate starting.

TRIALS — Competition with emphasis on skill over rough terrain.

TUNER — Usually the chief mechanic for a racer.

TWO-STROKE — A motorcycle which has a power stroke with each revolution of the engine.

UNDERSQUARE — Engine with stroke larger than bore.

WHOOP-DE-DOOS — A continuous series of dips and rises in rapid succession.

WRENCH — A mechanic or pit crew member.

Some classic trials bikes

Still revered by many as the greatest four-stroke single ever made, the BSA Gold Star in its trials version is now a collector's item. It was used by the factory's full-time works team, which included Jeff Smith, and can still be seen in action powering trials sidecar outfits. Versions of the same machine were produced for road racing and for moto-cross. Here the rider is Bill Nicholson in the 1951 Travers Trophy Trial

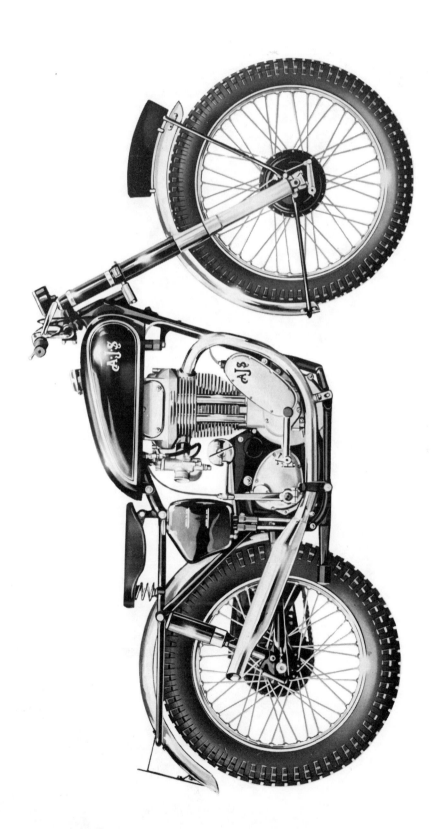

Lots of bottom-end power, a motor that wouldn't die even on the slightest whiff of throttle and the ability to find grip in the most slippery conditions, were the assets of the 350 cc AJS on which such greats as Gordon Jackson Hugh Viney made their names. But the big bikes were also heavy and when light two-strokes began to develop equal power, the writing was well and truly on the wall. This is a 1959 model 16C AJS

Perhaps the most famous individual trials bike ever - the 500 cc single-cylinder four-stroke Ariel which Sammy Miller campaigned before finally going over to a 250 cc two-stroke. GOV 132, on which Sammy won countless trials and titles, now rests in the Beaulieu Motor Museum in the Hampshire countryside. This photograph was taken in 1962

The ultimate in development of the Greeves trials machine. This was my specially-built lightweight 250 that took much of 1962 to prepare. I carved and shaved away at the bike and then polished or chromed what was left. It didn't win the Scottish - the event for which it was primarily built - but it was certainly the most sanitary machine in the entry

The machine which led the Spanish invasion which, for a time, virtually monopolised trials results - the 250 cc Bultaco Sherpa. Designed and developed by Sammy Miller after he finally discarded his 500 cc Ariel, the 'Taco started with four gears, went to five and then had its capacity increased to 325 cc. This is the 1964 model

The Montesa Cota which I designed and developed with the Spanish factory after leaving Greeves gave me the chance to put into practice many ideas which I had had for some years. It was an immediate success and monopolised the manufacturers' award in the all-important Scottish Six Days Trial - as well as giving me another European title during the first year with this experimental model. This is the first 5 speed Montesa in England in 1968

Third of the big Spanish companies based in Barcelona, Ossa used Derbyshire ace Mick Andrews to develop this 250 cc model which would have made a greater sales impact in Britain, at that time, but for a rather poor marketing set up and other difficulties. This is Mick Andrew's 1970 Scottish Six Days winning bike

The first Japanese bike to win the Scottish Six Days Trial was a 250 cc Yamaha ridden by Mick Andrews, but that was a highly specialised factory development machine with hosts of experimental features including cantilever suspension and a form of fuel injection to the single-cylinder, two-stroke engine. This is the 1974 production machine designated the TY 250

Suzuki, too, got in early with a machine, recognising the importance of the trials leisure machine market. This two-fifty was developed by ex-Greeves and Triumph works rider Gordon Farley. He started riding the bike in late 1973 and production versions were on the market a little over a year later. This, the production version, is the Suzuki RL 250

The first Kawasaki trials bike was this 450 cc model which I designed in my East London workshops. Like all prototypes, it had its faults but paved the way to the current generation of machines. Even in its experimental state it was able to win the 500 cc class of the 1973 Scottish Six Days Trial - its first competition outing

The 'unsurprising' news of 1974 was that Sammy Miller had signed a contract with Honda to develop their range of trials machines. Honda, of course, had already established itself in the four stroke trial market and could see the growth of trials. This is the first Honda 250 trials prototype brought into England featuring obvious Sammy Miller influence. This bike must herald the return of the four stroke trials bike

Postscript

   With any luck, you've enjoyed this book and are now thinking of a trip to your local dealer to buy your very first trials bike.

   Don't be apprehensive. You're not acquiring anything that will tax your mechanical know-how, even if you are zero-rated and have trouble turning on a fuel tap.

   Obviously, the newer the machine you buy the less maintenance you will be called on to do. Don't worry, either, that any new-found enthusiasm will quickly wane. When I ran a motorcycle showroom in London I found that less than 1 per cent of my first-time customers did not take to the sport and dropped out.

   Go for a modern bike from a factory in which you have confidence. That way you know that it is up to the job in hand and that the work you will have to do to keep it that way will be minimal. In fact remember my first instruction to Kawasaki's engineers and designers was **Produce a trials motorcycle that requires as much maintenance as a set of golf clubs.**

   Well that's it. If you are new to the game, I hope this book will provide you with a fresh interest. If you are already a trials rider, I trust that you will have found something which will enable you to get even more from this sport of ours.